ON PRAYER AND CONTEMPLATION

ON PRAYER AND CONTEMPLATION
Classic and Contemporary Texts

Edited by
Matthew Levering

A SHEED & WARD BOOK

ROWMAN & LITTLEFIELD PUBLISHERS, INC.
Lanham • Boulder • New York • Toronto • Oxford

A SHEED & WARD BOOK

ROWMAN & LITTLEFIELD PUBLISHERS, INC.

Published in the United States of America
by Rowman & Littlefield Publishers, Inc.
A wholly owned subsidiary of The Rowman & Littlefield Publishing Group, Inc.
4501 Forbes Boulevard, Suite 200, Lanham, Maryland 20706
www.rowmanlittlefield.com

PO Box 317
Oxford
OX2 9RU, UK

British Library Cataloguing in Publication Information Available

Library of Congress Cataloging-in-Publication Data

On prayer and contemplation : classic and contemporary texts / edited by Matthew
Levering.
        p. cm.
    "A Sheed & Ward book."
    Includes bibliographical references and index.
    ISBN 0-7425-4250-5 (alk. paper) — ISBN 0-7425-4251-3 (pbk. : alk. paper)
  1. Prayer—Catholic Church. 2. Prayer—Christianity. 3. Contemplation. I.
Levering, Matthew Webb, 1971– II. Title.

    BV210.3.06 2005
    248.3—dc22
                                                                    2004023620

Printed in the United States of America

∞™ The paper used in this publication meets the minimum requirements of
American National Standard for Information Sciences—Permanence of Paper
for Printed Library Materials, ANSI/NISO Z39.48-1992.

To Patty Levering and Ann Moretz,

Women of Prayer

Contents

Introduction

RECENTLY, A FRIEND WROTE TO ME to ask how I found time for prayer. She asked specifically what practices of prayer and contemplation I included in my daily routine. I wrote back and listed what I generally did in a typical week. I soon regretted having given such an enumeration, however, because my friend replied that it seemed too bad that I did not do "X" on a daily basis.

Mixed with some short-lived irritation over my friend presuming to take on the role of spiritual director, was a sense that I *would* like to pray more. After all, prayer, as communion with God, is the foundation for everything that lasts. It is through prayer and worship that we are trained to turn away from our cleaving to things that are passing away and instead learn to love eternal realities, in light of which the things of this world have their real and lasting meaning.

I once witnessed an older man, dear to me, approaching death. He had been in failing health for more than a year, since his wife had died. He still was able to live at home, thanks to the assistance of his son. He was experiencing severe incontinence, so the doctors decided to operate on his slow-growing prostate cancer. This operation was a success: the cancer was removed. The day after the surgery, when I went to visit my friend, he was his old self, full of enthusiasm for the future, for a life of renewed vigor. And yet, as we soon discovered, he could not *recover* from the surgery. As the weeks passed, his body remained far too weak for him to care for himself.

His son had the terrible task of informing his father that he, the father, would be moved not back to his beloved home, but to a nursing home for round-the-clock care—a very nice nursing home, where he was known in the local community and had friends, but a nursing home nonetheless. Even before this news, my friend regained the waxen, sunken, dying look that he had had before the surgery and that had lifted only in that one moment of earthly *hope* when he thought that he felt his strength returning and that he would return home to his beloved mountain.

I saw my friend once more after the move to the nursing home. It was not that he was without family; he was not alone, his children were around. By that time, his mind was beginning to whirl, but what emerged, when his mind cleared, was tremendous anger and despair at the absolute, unimaginable gulf that he now faced. As he said, "I will soon be nothing, forever." He had told me earlier, while still in good health, that although faith was important for good moral action, he did not believe in God. There was no heaven, because when they had sent Sputnik and the various probes into outer space, they could find no signs of heaven.

Within a couple of weeks, my friend, taking control and asserting his dignity in the only way he knew how, refused to eat for a couple of days and died—"peacefully."

Each of us is confronted not only with dying, whether our own or that of our loved ones, but with other crises. At such moments, we will either have the resources to draw ourselves, and others, closer to the reality of God who is not "passing away" and who loves us and has intended us to love him; or we will lack those resources. Prayer is the point of contact, the foundation for true resources in this world.

As T. S. Eliot put it, we must seek to find ourselves: "At the still point of the turning world. Neither flesh nor / fleshless; / Neither from nor towards; at the still point, there the dance / is, / But neither arrest nor movement. And do not call it fixity, / Where past and future are gathered. Neither movement from nor towards, / Neither ascent nor decline. Except for the point, the still / point, / There would be no dance, and there is only the dance."[1]

It sometimes seems, however, that prayer is not for us. Prayer is for better people; prayer is for people who have more faith than we do and who are on a higher spiritual plane; prayer is for holier-than-thou types full of smug security; prayer is for people who want to be challenged to conform to God's call to holiness, which we do not.

And yet, could it be that prayer is a more *this-worldly* activity than one might at first imagine? I recall my most vivid early experience of prayer. On a ski trip when I was a boy, our car slid off the icy, traffic-filled mountain road in the dark—but no one was hurt. We stayed at a motel that night, and my father pulled out the Gideon's Bible. He read from it and we prayed gratefully.

Another time came when I was twenty years old. Due to complications from an orthopedic surgery a few years before, a sharp sliver of bone inside my leg punctured (an ever-so-small puncture) my artery. The pain quickly subsided into a throbbing, and, though slightly hobbled, I ignored the pain. I had a trip coming up, a vacation in the Swiss Alps and a month-long tour of parts of Europe, which I did not want to miss. After a few days of hiking in the Alps, I noticed a small spot of blood forming on the side of my right foot, like a bruise. It kept increasing. In Annecy, France, I went to the emergency room of a small hospital. After learning the seriousness of the situation, I recall praying, in a state of fear, and suddenly experiencing waves of profound assurance—a firm awareness that God was present and working in this situation. I did not know if I would live or die, but I knew suddenly that God was actively present.

Two years later, having graduated from college, I had another set of experiences that affected my perspective on prayer. The first came after I had decided to try to become a novelist. After a couple months of writing drafts dealing with the issue of faith, I posed to myself the questions that my "characters" were asking: Is faith possible? Does God exist?

The answer struck me with a terribly sinking heart: No, God doesn't exist. Why should he? And because God doesn't exist, I will soon be *nothing* for eternity, entirely obliterated.

For three days I got up and did my usual things—feeling exactly like a living dead man. It was an experience of death-in-life, of a profoundly sad resignation. It was a feeling of death-in-*life*, because I could still easily go about my daily tasks. It was not a paralyzing, clinical depression. Rather, it was like looking around on a sunny day, appreciating the sun and yet knowing, as if it were in a wound at the core of my heart, that all these appearances were concealing—barely concealing—the rush of senseless nothingness, endless obliteration.

On the fourth day, I went to the library of Duke Divinity School, looking for any books that might give any indication that God existed. I wanted to at least learn the case for God, if indeed there was any case beyond novelistic depictions of the human condition. That day, I studied my first theology and, thanks be to God, began to hope again.

The second experience occurred within a year. I found myself facing another operation—this time for what seemed to be a pinched nerve in my back. The doctors did some exploratory procedure that required taking spinal fluid. I was supposed to recover quickly but instead found that for a few days I could not get up without feeling dizzy and having to lie back down immediately—the spine was not sealing properly. I recall feeling irrational fear, as if I would be like that for my entire life. I remember a powerful sense of wanting to be prayed for, of wanting other people's prayer and to be located within a circle of prayer.

In the Bible, King Hezekiah, the great king of Judah who held off the Assyrian Empire in the eighth century BC becomes sick and is near death. His example is instructive:

> Isaiah the prophet the son of Amoz came to him, and said to him, "Thus says the Lord, 'Set your house in order; for you shall die, you shall not recover.'" Then Hezekiah turned his face to the wall, and prayed to the Lord, saying, "Remember now, O Lord, I beseech thee, how I have walked before thee in faithfulness and with a whole heart, and have done what is good in thy sight." And Hezekiah wept bitterly. (2 Kings 20:1–3)

If the prophet Isaiah came to you as your chaplain and informed you that now was the time to prepare for death, it might seem that you would accept it as a divinely ordained thing and would put yourself resignedly and completely in God's hands. But note what Hezekiah does. He prays with bitter and profound tears!

The point is that prayer is not just for elevated, otherworldly souls. Prayer is a practice of this-worldly regular human beings who have no grounds for holier-than-thou mentalities. Prayer and the desire for prayer belong to the necessary rhythms of meaningful life.

Jesus Christ tells a parable that depicts the humility of true prayer:

> Two men went up into the temple to pray, one a Pharisee and the other a tax collector. The Pharisee stood and prayed thus with himself, "God, I thank thee that I am not like other men, extortioners, unjust, adulterers, or even like this tax collector. I fast twice a week, I give tithes of all that I get." But the tax collector, standing far off, would not even lift up his eyes to heaven, but beat his breast, saying, "God, be merciful to me a sinner!" (Luke 18:10–13)

Jesus comments on this parable, "I tell you, this man [the tax collector] went down to his house justified rather than the other; for every one who exalts himself will be humbled, but he who humbles himself will be exalted" (Luke 18:14). Indeed, prayer is for sinners; prayer is for people who are in trouble; and we are *all* in this condition. We need God's presence, strength, and grace to lift us up. Prayer, then, is hardly reserved for those who imagine themselves—or whom we imagine—to be perfect, the elite, the holier-than-thou. Prayer is for those who, by God's grace, recognize themselves to be in trouble, in need of divine help.

In the Church, we gather together to offer up, in, with, and through Christ the prayer of those who profoundly need God's mercy and love. Such prayer, offered as a community, becomes our own when united to daily practices of personal prayer, in which we ask God to turn our mind and heart to himself.

The practice of prayer reorients our lives from having foundations only in things that are passing away—things that we are going to lose—to having foundations in God. In God, the things of this world have meaning; without God, the things of this world would be nothing more than thin coverings that open up to reveal the horror of empty and everlasting nothingness. God does exist. But his true existence can only be personally experienced in prayer, because only in prayer can we let go of our fearful insistence on being in "control" (our self-centered lives, which are always collapsing) and enter into the reality of God's demanding and consoling presence (God-centered lives).

Jesus invites us to establish our lives upon the foundation of communion with Jesus in prayer, which must include conversion of our whole being, reordering ourselves toward holy actions. The life of prayer includes the elements of trust, simplicity or detachment from worldly possessions, worship, and fellowship with the body of believers.

At the conclusion of the Sermon on the Mount, in which Jesus instructs us in the radical life of self-giving love, he teaches, "Every one then who hears these words of mine and does them will be like a wise man who built his house upon the rock; and the rain fell, and the floods came, and the winds blew and beat upon that house, but it did not fall, because it had been founded on the rock" (Matthew 7:24–25). Only communion in prayer with the living God, revealed in Christ, provides this "rock" that endures trials.

As weak people, we can admit our great need for God's presence. We can learn to follow Jesus' advice not to be anxious above all for health, food, clothes, and shelter, but rather above all to seek communion with God. If we learn to pray, however poorly, we will be following Jesus'

admonition: "But seek first his [God's] kingdom and his righteousness, and all these things shall be yours as well" (Matthew 6:33).

When we try to learn to pray, however, we find that we cannot separate learning how to pray *from Jesus,* from learning how to pray *with and
from those who have themselves learned from Jesus.* The great Christian
teachers and saints have demonstrated by their lives how profoundly
they have learned from Jesus, and they can therefore assist us in learning from Jesus about how to pray in "the fellowship of the Holy Spirit"
(2 Corinthians 13:14).

It is only in this fellowship, which is the communion of saints, that we
experience the full relational depths of prayer. As St. Paul proclaims,
"When we cry, 'Abba! Father!' it is the Spirit himself bearing witness
with our spirit that we are children of God, and if children, then heirs,
heirs of God and fellow heirs with Christ, provided we suffer with him
in order that we may also be glorified with him" (Romans 8:15–17). All
creation prays together for fulfillment in God, and our prayers in Christ
join us to this fellowship: "We know that the whole creation has been
groaning in travail together until now; and not only creation, but we
ourselves who have the first fruits of the Spirit groan inwardly as we wait
for adoption as sons, the redemption of our bodies" (Romans 8:22–23).

Furthermore, we do not need to rely on our own strength, or our own
goodness, to belong to this communion of prayer. St. Paul reminds us,
"Likewise the Spirit helps us in our weakness, for we do not know how
to pray as we ought, but the Spirit himself intercedes for us with sighs
too deep for words" (Romans 8:26).

The present volume thus explores the life of "sighs too deep for
words," the *life of prayer,* by means of excerpts from the writings of fifteen great saints and teachers of the Church, spanning the 2,000 years of
Christian history. We begin with three authors from the first centuries of
the Church's existence; in these three texts, we are reminded especially of
the communal aspect of prayer. St. Clement, bishop of Rome in the first
century, offers a beautiful prayer of supplication to God for the unity of
the Church in Corinth, which was beset by division. St. Justin Martyr,
writing in the second century, describes the prayers of the early Christian liturgy, whose pinnacle is the Eucharist. Egeria, a pilgrim to
Jerusalem in the early 300s, offers a marvelously detailed eyewitness account of the celebration of Holy Week by the Church in Jerusalem. From
the pinnacle of the Patristic period (third–eighth centuries) we find

three great teachers of personal prayer. St. Gregory of Nyssa, a fourth-century bishop and theologian known for his mystical writings, expounds on what he calls the "good work of prayer," which requires our care and attention just as do other daily tasks. John Cassian, who trained in Egypt as a monk in the fourth century and brought this monastic wisdom to the Latin-speaking world, describes four kinds of prayer and comments on each verse of the Lord's Prayer, thereby providing a masterful introduction to the life of prayer. The fifth-century bishop and theological master St. Augustine presents a biblical commentary on Christ's Sermon on the Mount, from which I have excerpted his beautiful discussion of the Lord's Prayer.

Each of the three texts I have selected from the medieval period (eighth–fifteenth centuries) presents a different aspect of the experience of contemplative prayer. The great thirteenth-century theologian St. Thomas Aquinas explores the mystical experience of "rapture" that may occur at the height of prayer. St. Gregory of Sinai, a monk at Mount Athos in the early fourteenth century, depicts the process of entering into the divine stillness, aided by the chanting of psalms. St. Catherine of Siena, who battled in the late fourteenth century to persuade the pope to return to Rome rather than remain in residence at Avignon, emphasizes that the key to prayer is loving desire for God, through which vocal prayer will rise to the level of mental, or contemplative, prayer.

Similar wisdom for those who seek to pray is found in the writings of the three saints representative of the post-Reformation period (sixteenth–eighteenth centuries). All three are from the amazing sixteenth century: one was the founder of the Jesuits and two were reformers of the Carmelite order in Spain. All three inspire us to attempt greater heights in our life of prayer and to commune more profoundly with God.

St. Ignatius of Loyola, who founded the Jesuits after renouncing a career in the military, is best known for his Spiritual Exercises, a four-week spiritual course still given all over the world. I have selected his instructions to the person giving the Exercises, the retreat master or spiritual director; these instructions reveal a keen sense for the development of the God-centered life. St. Teresa, the great Carmelite reformer and foundress, depicts a stage in the spiritual marriage of God and the soul that comes about through a lifetime of prayer. St. John of the Cross, the mystical poet whose spiritual and theological depth makes him among the greatest theologians of the Church's history, interprets a section from his poem on the "dark night of the soul." He teaches us that at a high level of prayer, the soul is conformed to Christ's suffering and purged of its cleaving to worldly things through a period of mystical darkness without the normal consolations that pertain to the heights of the contemplative life.

The last three selections, from the modern period (nineteenth century to the present), exhort us to desire the life of prayer. Blessed John Henry Newman, a nineteenth-century English theologian who received the honor of being named a cardinal of the Catholic Church, calls on his listeners, in a sermon delivered early in his career, to recognize personal and communal prayer as both a daily duty and a privilege that constitutes true freedom. Blessed Elizabeth of the Trinity, who died early in the twentieth century, offers a ten-day spiritual retreat that witnesses to her teaching that in the life of prayer she has found "Heaven on earth." St. Edith Stein, a Jewish convert, philosopher, and theologian who was killed by the Nazis in the Holocaust, explores the communal prayer of the Body of Christ, the Church, as flowing from the communal prayer of Israel.

The Letter to the Hebrews teaches:

> Therefore, since we are surrounded by so great a cloud of witnesses, let us also lay aside every weight, and sin which clings so closely, and let us run with perseverance the race that is set before us, looking to Jesus the pioneer and perfecter of our faith, who for the joy that was set before him endured the cross, despising the shame, and is seated at the right hand of God. (Hebrews 12:1–2)

The author of Hebrews is encouraging his audience to endure the trials and persecutions that confront them rather than to renounce their faith. His words, however, speak to us today as well. We are indeed "surrounded by a great cloud of witnesses."

Rather than despairing of ever coming to know God, let us, therefore, by means of the communal (liturgical) and personal practices of prayer *passed on to us by the saints and teachers of the Church*, strive to build our lives upon the *rock* of prayerful communion in Christ Jesus.

Note

1. T. S. Eliot, "Burnt Norton," in *Four Quartets* (New York: Harcourt, 1943).

St. Clement of Rome

St. Clement, third bishop of Rome, wrote this letter in the 90s AD. Writing to the Corinthian Church, he uses his authority as bishop of the Church in Rome and his profound understanding of the gospel to entreat certain schismatic members of the Corinthian Church to return to the fold. The following excerpt from the letter is a lengthy prayer to God, the Father, through Christ, the Son. St. Clement pleads with God, the Creator of the world, for the grace of forgiveness and the grace of concord that build up the Church. He prays that the schismatic members of the Corinthian Church will return to a true understanding of the authority that God has bestowed on the bishops of the Church, an authority that both fosters ecclesial unity and enables believers to imitate the obedience of Christ.

B UT SHOULD ANY DISOBEY WHAT HAS been said by Him through us, let them understand that they will entangle themselves in transgression and no small danger. But for our part we shall be innocent of this sin, and will offer earnest prayer and supplication that the Creator of the universe may preserve undiminished the established number of His

Excerpts from *The Epistles of St. Clement of Rome and St. Ignatius of Antioch*, from Ancient Christian Writers, vol. 1, translated and annotated by James A. Kleist, S.J., Ph.D., 45–49. Copyright © 1946 by Rev. Johannes Quasten and Rev. Joseph C. Plumpe, Paulist Press, Inc., New York/Mahwah, N.J. Used with permission of Paulist Press. www.paulistpress.com.

elect in all the world through His beloved Son Jesus Christ, through whom He has called us *out of darkness into light*, out of ignorance into the full knowledge of the splendor of His name that we may hope in Thy name which gave existence to all creation. Open *the eyes of our heart*, that we may know Thee who alone art *Highest among the highest and Holy, reposing among the holy; who humblest the pride of the haughty, destroyest the designs of the heathens; who raisest up the lowly and humblest the lofty, makest rich and makest poor, slayest and bringest to life;* who alone art the Benefactor *of spirits and the God of all flesh. Thou gazest upon the deep*, Thou beholdest the works of men, the Helper in danger, *the savior in despair*, the Creator and Watcher of every spirit. Thou multipliest the nations upon the earth, and from among all Thou hast chosen those that love Thee through Jesus Christ, Thy beloved Son, through whom Thou hast instructed, sanctified, and honored us. We beg Thee, O Master, to be our *Helper and Protector*: deliver those of us who are in distress, raise up the fallen, show Thy face to those in need, heal the infirm, bring back the erring of Thy people, feed the hungry, ransom our prisoners, set the infirm upon their feet, comfort the fainthearted: *let all the nations know that Thou art the only God*, that Jesus Christ is Thy Son, *that we are Thy people and the sheep of Thy pasture.*

For Thou hast made known the everlasting constitution of the world through *the forces at work in it.* Thou, O Lord, hast created the world, Thou who art faithful in all generations, right in Thy judgments, wonderful in strength and transcendent greatness, wise in creating, and judicious in establishing what has come into being, beneficent throughout the visible world and kind toward those that trust in Thee. *O merciful and compassionate one*, forgive us our iniquities and misdemeanors and transgressions and short-comings! Do not consider every sin of Thy servants and servant maids; but cleanse us as only Thy truth can cleanse, and *direct our steps to walk in holiness of heart and to do the things which are good and pleasing in Thy sight* and in the sight of our rulers. Yes, Master, *let Thy face beam upon us*, that we may do good in peace and be sheltered *under Thy mighty hand* and delivered from every sin *by Thy uplifted arm*, and deliver us from such as hate us without cause. Grant concord and peace to us as well as to all the inhabitants of the earth, just as Thou didst grant it to our fathers when they piously *called upon Thee in faith and truth*; grant us to be obedient to Thy almighty and glorious name, as well as to our princes and rulers on earth.

Thou, O Master, through Thy transcendent and indescribable sovereignty hast given them the power of royalty, so that we, acknowledging the honor and glory conferred upon them by Thee, may bow to them, without in the least opposing Thy will. Grant to them, O Lord, health, peace, concord, and firmness, so that they may without hindrance exercise the supreme leadership Thou hast conferred on them. For it is Thou, O Master, O heavenly *King of all ages*, that conferrest upon the sons of men glory and honor and authority over the things which are upon the earth. Do Thou, O Lord, direct their counsels in accord with what is *good and pleasing in Thy sight*, so that they may piously exercise in peace and gentleness the authority Thou hast granted them, and thus experience Thy graciousness. To Thee, who alone art able to bestow these and even greater blessings upon us, we render thanks and praise through the High Priest and Ruler of our souls, Jesus Christ, through whom be to Thee the glory and majesty now and for all generations and forever and evermore. Amen.

What we have written to you, brethren, sufficiently explains what concerns our worship and is most helpful for a virtuous life to those who wish to live piously and dutifully. For, concerning faith and repentance and genuine charity and self-control and sobriety and patient endurance—we have touched upon every subject, and reminded you that you are in duty bound to please Almighty God through piety and truth and long-suffering: you are to live in concord, without bearing malice, in love and peace, joined to constant forbearance. In this manner our forbears, mentioned above, were acceptable and cherished a humble frame of mind toward the Father and God and Creator and all mankind. And we have all the more pleasure in recalling this to your memory because we are well aware that we are writing to persons who are *believers* and highly distinguished and deeply versed in the writings that contain God's educative revelation.

It is right, therefore, that we should adhere to so many and such notable examples and bow the neck and discharge the duty of obedience, so that, ceasing from that futile dissension, we may without any blame reach the goal set before us in truth. You certainly will give us the keenest pleasure if you prove obedient to what we have written through the Holy Spirit, and extirpate the lawless passion of your jealousy in accordance with the pleas we have made in this letter for peace and concord. We are sending trustworthy and prudent men, who have led blameless lives among us from youth to old age, that they may be witnesses between you and us. We do this to make you feel that our whole care has been, and is, directed toward establishing speedy peace in your midst.

And now may the all-seeing God and Master *of spirits* and Lord *of all flesh*, who chose the Lord Jesus Christ and us through Him to be *a people set apart for Himself*, grant to every soul that invokes His transcendent and holy name—faith, fear, peace, patient endurance and long-suffering, self-control, holiness, and sobriety, so that they may be well-pleasing to His Majesty through our High Priest and Ruler, Jesus Christ, through whom be to Him glory and greatness, power and honor, both now and forever and evermore. Amen.

As for our representatives Claudius Ephebus and Valerius Bito, accompanied by Fortunatus, send them back to us at an early convenience, full of peace and joy, that they may without delay bring tidings of peace and concord—the object of our most ardent desires—and that we in turn may without delay rejoice in your tranquility.

May the grace of our Lord Jesus Christ be with you and with all that have anywhere in the world been called by God and through Him, through whom be to Him glory and honor and power and majesty and everlasting dominion, from eternity to eternity. Amen.

Questions

1. For what does St. Clement pray?
2. Note how St. Clement combines praise of God as Creator with praise of God as Redeemer. How does this connection shape the effect of his prayer?
3. What are the virtues consistent with Christian prayer, according to Clement?

St. Justin Martyr

St. Justin Martyr was born in Shechem, an ancient and biblically sig-
nificant city that had belonged to the Northern Kingdom of Israel
but that, under Roman rule, had received the name "Flavia Neapo-
lis." As a young man, Justin studied philosophy at Ephesus, where he
became a teacher of Platonist philosophy. After converting to Christianity, he moved to Rome and taught Christian philosophy, publishing several important writings in defense of the Christian faith.
For professing Christianity, he was martyred in Rome in 165. The
following excerpt gives one a sense of Christian liturgical prayer,
specifically the celebration of the liturgy of the Eucharist, in the
Church in Rome in the mid-second century. Prayer is never, for the
Christian, solely a solitary act; rather, the community gathers together to unite its prayers to the Father in the Son through the Holy
Spirit.

B UT WE, AFTER WE HAVE THUS WASHED him who has been convinced and
has assented to our teaching, bring him to the place where those
who are called brethren are assembled, in order that we may offer hearty
prayers in common for ourselves and for the baptized [illuminated] person, and for all others in every place, that we may be counted worthy,

From *The First Apology*, trans. Alexander Roberts and James Donaldson, in
Ante-Nicene Fathers, vol. 1: *The Apostolic Fathers, Justin Martyr, Irenaeus*
(Peabody, Mass.: Hendrickson, 1995 [1885]), 185–86.

now that we have learned the truth, by our works also to be found good citizens and keepers of the commandments, so that we may be saved with an everlasting salvation. Having ended the prayers, we salute one another with a kiss. There is then brought to the president of the brethren bread and a cup of wine mixed with water; and he taking them, gives praise and glory to the Father of the universe, through the name of the Son and of the Holy Ghost, and offers thanks at considerable length for our being counted worthy to receive these things at His hands. And when he has concluded the prayers and thanksgivings, all the people present express their assent by saying Amen. This word Amen answers in the Hebrew language to γέυσιτσ [so be it]. And when the president has given thanks, and all the people have expressed their assent, those who are called by us deacons give to each of those present to partake of the bread and wine mixed with water over which the thanksgiving was pronounced, and to those who are absent they carry away a portion.

And this food is called among us Εὐχαριστία [the Eucharist], of which no one is allowed to partake but the man who believes that the things which we teach are true, and who has been washed with the washing that is for the remission of sins, and unto regeneration, and who is so living as Christ has enjoined. For not as common bread and common drink do we receive these; but in like manner as Jesus Christ our Saviour, having been made flesh by the Word of God, had both flesh and blood for our salvation, so likewise have we been taught that the food which is blessed by the prayer of His word, and from which our blood and flesh by transmutation are nourished, is the flesh and blood of that Jesus who was made flesh. For the apostles, in the memoirs composed by them, which are called Gospels, have thus delivered unto us what was enjoined upon them; that Jesus took bread, and when He had given thanks, said, "This do in remembrance of Me, this is My body"; and that, after the same manner, having taken the cup and given thanks, He said, "This is My blood"; and gave it to them alone. Which the wicked devils have imitated in the mysteries of Mithras, commanding the same thing to be done. For, that bread and a cup of water are placed with certain incantations in the mystic rites of one who is being initiated, you either know or can learn.

And we afterwards continually remind each other of these things. And the wealthy among us help the needy; and we always keep together; and for all things wherewith we are supplied, we bless the Maker of all through His Son Jesus Christ, and through the Holy Ghost. And on the day called Sunday, all who live in cities or in the country gather together to one place, and the memoirs of the apostles or the writings of the prophets are read, as long as time permits; then, when the reader has ceased, the president verbally instructs, and exhorts to the imitation of these good things. Then we all rise together and pray, and, as we before said, when our prayer is ended, bread and wine and water are brought, and the president in the like manner offers prayers and thanksgivings, according to his ability, and the people assent, saying Amen; and there is a distribution to each, and a participation of that over which thanks have been given, and to those who are absent a portion is sent by the deacons. And they who are well to do, and willing, give what each thinks fit; and what is collected is deposited with the president, who succours the orphans and widows, and those who, through sickness or any other cause, are in want, and those who are in bonds, and the strangers so-journing among us, and in a word takes care of all who are in need. But Sunday is the day on which we all hold our common assembly, because it is the first day on which God, having wrought a change in the darkness and matter, made the world; and Jesus Christ our Saviour on the same day rose from the dead. For He was crucified on the day before that of Saturn (Saturday); and on the day after that of Saturn, which is the day of the Sun, having appeared to His apostles and disciples, He taught them these things, which we have submitted to you also for your consideration.

Questions

1. Why is common, not merely personal, prayer so valued by St. Justin?
2. Describe the liturgy of the Eucharist according to St. Justin.
3. What are the fruits of the community's liturgical life of prayer?

Egeria

In the mid-fourth century, Egeria, a member of a religious community of women, made a pilgrimage to the Holy Land. Her record of her experiences, intended for her community, is a priceless depiction of the liturgical prayer that characterized the Church in Jerusalem at this time. Egeria arrived in Jerusalem while St. Cyril of Jerusalem was bishop and when the great church in Jerusalem, funded by Emperor Constantine, was still new. The fourth century marked one of the high points of Christian pilgrimage to Jerusalem. Egeria provides a detailed account of the public prayers and liturgies of Holy Week and reminds us how central communal prayer is to the Christian understanding of prayer and contemplation.

THE FOLLOWING DAY, SUNDAY, marks the beginning of Holy Week, which they call here the Great Week. On this Sunday morning, at the completion of those rites which are customarily celebrated at the Anastasis or the Cross from the first cockcrow until dawn, everyone assembles for the liturgy according to custom in the major church, called the Martyrium. It is called the Martyrium because it is on Golgotha, behind

Excerpts from *Egeria: Diary of a Pilgrimage*, from Ancient Christian Writers, no. 38, translated and annotated by George E. Gingras, Ph.D., 103–16. Copyright © 1970 by Rev. Johannes Quasten and Rev. Walter J. Burghardt, S.J., and Thomas Comerford Lawler, The Newman Press, N.Y./Mahwah, N.J. Used with permission of Paulist Press. www.paulistpress.com.

the Cross, where the Lord suffered His Passion, and is therefore a shrine of martyrdom. As soon as everything has been celebrated in the major church as usual, but before the dismissal is given, the archdeacon raises his voice and first says: "Throughout this whole week, beginning tomorrow at the ninth hour, let us all gather in the Martyrium, in the major church." Then he raises his voice a second time, saying: "Today let us all be ready to assemble at the seventh hour at the Eleona." When the dismissal has been given in the Martyrium or major church, the bishop is led to the accompaniment of hymns to the Anastasis, and there all ceremonies are accomplished which customarily take place every Sunday at the Anastasis following the dismissal from the Martyrium. Then everyone retires to his home to eat hastily, so that at the beginning of the seventh hour everyone will be ready to assemble in the church on the Eleona, by which I mean the Mount of Olives, where the grotto in which the Lord taught is located.

At the seventh hour all the people go up to the church on the Mount of Olives, that is, to the Eleona. The bishop sits down, hymns and antiphons appropriate to the day and place are sung, and there are likewise readings from the Scriptures. As the ninth hour approaches, they move up, chanting hymns, to the Imbomon, that is, to the place from which the Lord ascended into heaven; and everyone sits down there. When the bishop is present, the people are always commanded to be seated, so that only the deacons remain standing. And there hymns and antiphons proper to the day and place are sung, interspersed with appropriate readings from the Scriptures and prayers.

As the eleventh hour draws near, that particular passage from Scripture is read in which the children bearing palms and branches came forth to meet the Lord, saying: *Blessed is He who comes in the name of the Lord.* The bishop and all the people rise immediately, and then everyone walks down from the top of the Mount of Olives, with the people preceding the bishop and responding continually with *Blessed is He who comes in the name of the Lord* to the hymns and antiphons. All the children who are present here, including those who are not yet able to walk because they are too young and therefore are carried on their parents' shoulders, all of them bear branches, some carrying palms, others, olive branches. And the bishop is led in the same manner as the Lord once was led. From the top of the mountain as far as the Anastasis, everyone accompanies the bishop the whole way on foot, and this includes distinguished ladies and men of consequence, reciting the responses all the while; and they move very slowly so that the people will not tire. By the time they arrive at the Anastasis, it is already evening. Once they have arrived there, even though it is evening, vespers is celebrated; then a prayer is said at the Cross and the people are dismissed.

On Monday, the following day, they carry out in the Anastasis whatever ceremonies are customarily performed from the first cockcrow until dawn, as well as whatever is done at the third and sixth hours throughout Lent. However, at the ninth hour everyone comes together in the major church or Martyrium, and until the first hour of the night they continually sing hymns and antiphons, and read passages from the Scriptures fitting to the day and the place, always interrupting them with prayers. Vespers is celebrated in the Martyrium, when the hour for it is at hand. The result is that it is already night when the dismissal is given at the Martyrium. As soon as the dismissal has been given, the bishop is led from there to the Anastasis to the accompaniment of hymns. When he has entered the Anastasis, a hymn is sung, a prayer is said, first the catechumens and then the faithful are blessed, and finally the dismissal is given.

On Tuesday they do everything in the same way as Monday. Only this is added on Tuesday: late at night, after the dismissal has been given in the Martyrium and they have gone to the Anastasis, and a second dismissal has been given at the Anastasis, they all go at that hour in the night to the church which is located on Mount Eleona. As soon as they have arrived in this church, the bishop goes into the grotto where the Lord used to teach His disciples. There the bishop takes up the book of the Gospels and, while standing, reads the words of the Lord which are written in the Gospel according to Matthew at the place where He said: *Take heed that no man seduce you.* Then the bishop reads the Lord's entire discourse. When he has finished reading it, he says a prayer and blesses the catechumens and then the faithful. The dismissal is given, and they return from the mountain, and everyone goes to his own home, for it is now very late at night.

On Wednesday everything is done throughout the day from the first cockcrow just as on Monday and Tuesday. However, following the dismissal at night at the Martyrium, the bishop is led to the accompaniment of hymns to the Anastasis. He goes immediately into the grotto within the Anastasis, and he stands within the railings. A priest, however, standing in front of the railings, takes up the Gospel and reads that passage where

Judas Iscariot went to the Jews to set the price they would pay him to betray the Lord. While this passage is being read, there is such moaning and groaning from among the people that no one can help being moved to tears in that moment. Afterwards, a prayer is said, first the catechumens and then the faithful are blessed, and finally the dismissal is given.

On Thursday whatever is customarily done from the first cockcrow until morning and what is done at the third and sixth hours takes place at the Anastasis. At the eighth hour all the people gather as usual at the Martyrium, earlier, however, than on other days, because the dismissal must be given more quickly. When all the people have assembled, the prescribed rites are celebrated. On that day the sacrifice is offered at the Martyrium, and the dismissal from there is given around the tenth hour. Before the dismissal is given, however, the archdeacon raises his voice, saying: "At the first hour of the night let us assemble at the church which is on the Eleona, for much toil lies ahead of us on this day's night." Following the dismissal from the Martyrium, everyone proceeds behind the Cross, where, after a hymn is sung and a prayer is said, the bishop offers the sacrifice and everyone receives Communion. Except on this one day, throughout the year the sacrifice is never offered behind the Cross save on this day alone. The dismissal is given there, and everyone goes to the Anastasis, where a prayer is said, the catechumens as well as the faithful are blessed, as is customary, and the dismissal is given.

Everyone then hurries home to eat, because, immediately after having eaten, everyone goes to the Eleona, to the church where the grotto in which the Lord gathered with His disciples on that day is located. And there, until around the fifth hour of the night, they continually sing hymns and antiphons and read the scriptural passages proper to the place and to the day. Between these, prayers are said. Moreover, they read those passages from the Gospels in which the Lord spoke to His disciples on that day while sitting in the same grotto which lies within this church. And from here, around the sixth hour of the night, everyone goes up to the Imbomon, singing hymns. That is the place from which the Lord ascended into heaven. There also they sing hymns and antiphons and read scriptural passages proper to the day; and whatever prayers are said, whatever prayers the bishop recites, they will always be proper to the day and to the place.

As soon as it begins to be the hour of cockcrow, everyone comes down from the Imbomon singing hymns and proceeds toward the very place where the Lord prayed, as it is written in the Gospel: *And He went as far as a stone's throw and He prayed*, and so forth. On that spot stands a tasteful church. The bishop and all the people enter there, where a prayer fitting to the day and the place is said, followed by an appropriate hymn, and a reading of that passage from the Gospel where He said to His disciples: *Watch, that you enter not into temptation*. The whole of this passage is read there, and a second prayer is then said. Next, everyone, including the smallest children, walk down from there to Gethsemani, accompanying the bishop with hymns. Singing hymns, they come to Gethsemani very slowly on account of the great multitude of people, who are fatigued by vigils and exhausted by the daily fasts, and because of the rather high mountain they have to descend. Over two hundred church candles are ready to provide light for all the people.

On arriving in Gethsemani a suitable prayer is first said, followed by a hymn, and then the passage from the Gospel describing the arrest of the Lord is read. During the reading of this passage there is such moaning and groaning with weeping from all the people that their moaning can be heard practically as far as the city. And from that hour everyone goes back on foot to the city singing hymns, and they arrive at the gate at the hour when men can begin to recognize one another. From there, throughout the center of the city, all without exception are ready at hand, the old and the young, the rich and the poor, everyone; and on this day especially no one withdraws from the vigil before early morning. It is in this fashion that the bishop is led from Gethsemani to the gate, and from there through the whole city to the Cross.

When they finally arrive before the Cross, it is already beginning to be broad daylight. There then is read the passage from the Gospel where the Lord is led before Pilate, and whatsoever words are written that Pilate spoke to the Lord or to the Jews, all this is read. Afterwards, the bishop addresses the people, comforting them, since they have labored the whole night and since they are to labor again on this day, admonishing them not to grow weary, but to have hope in God who will bestow great graces on them for their efforts. And comforting them as he can, he addresses them saying: "Go, for the time being, each of you, to your homes; sit there awhile, and around the second hour of the day let everyone be on hand here so that from that hour until the sixth hour you may see the holy wood of the cross, and thus believe that it was offered for the salvation of each and every one of us. From the sixth hour on we will have to assemble here, before the Cross, so that we may devote ourselves to prayers and scriptural readings until nightfall."

After this, following the dismissal from the Cross, which occurs before sunrise, everyone now stirred up goes immediately to Sion to pray at the pillar where the Lord was whipped. Returning from there then, everyone rests for a short time in his own house, and soon all are ready. A throne is set up for the bishop on Golgotha behind the Cross, which now stands there. The bishop sits on his throne, a table covered with a linen cloth is set before him, and the deacons stand around the table. The gilded silver casket containing the sacred wood of the cross is brought in and opened. Both the wood of the cross and the inscription are taken out and placed on the table. As soon as they have been placed on the table, the bishop, remaining seated, grips the ends of the sacred wood with his hands, while the deacons, who are standing about, keep watch over it. There is a reason why it is guarded in this manner. It is the practice here for all the people to come forth one by one, the faithful as well as the catechumens, to bow down before the table, kiss the holy wood, and then move on. It is said that someone (I do not know when) took a bite and stole a piece of the holy cross. Therefore, it is now guarded by the deacons standing around, lest there be anyone who would dare come and do that again.

All the people pass through one by one; all of them bow down, touching the cross and the inscription, first with their foreheads, then with their eyes; and, after kissing the cross, they move on. No one, however, puts out his hand to touch the cross. As soon as they have kissed the cross and passed on through, a deacon, who is standing, holds out the ring of Solomon and the phial with which the kings are anointed. They kiss the phial and venerate the ring from more or less the second hour; and thus until the sixth hour all the people pass through, entering through one door, exiting through another. All this occurs in the place where the day before, on Thursday, the sacrifice was offered.

When the sixth hour is at hand, everyone goes before the Cross, regardless of whether it is raining or whether it is hot. This place has no roof, for it is a sort of very large and beautiful courtyard lying between the Cross and the Anastasis. The people are so clustered together there that it is impossible for anything to be opened. A chair is placed for the bishop before the Cross, and from the sixth to the ninth hours nothing else is done except the reading of passages from Scripture.

First, whichever Psalms speak of the Passion are read. Next, there are readings from the apostles, either from the Epistles of the apostles or the Acts, wherever they speak of the Passion of the Lord. Next, the texts of the Passion from the Gospels are read. Then there are readings from the prophets, where they said that the Lord would suffer; and then they read from the Gospels, where He foretells the Passion. And so, from the sixth to the ninth hour, passages from Scripture are continuously read and hymns are sung, to show the people that whatever the prophets had said would come to pass concerning the Passion of the Lord can be shown, both through the Gospels and the writings of the apostles, to have taken place. And so, during those three hours, all the people are taught that nothing happened which was not first prophesied, and that nothing was prophesied which was not completely fulfilled. Prayers are continually interspersed, and the prayers themselves are proper to the day. At each reading and at every prayer, it is astonishing how much emotion and groaning there is from all the people. There is no one, young or old, who on this day does not sob more than can be imagined for the whole three hours, because the Lord suffered all this for us. After this, when the ninth hour is at hand, the passage is read from the Gospel according to Saint John where Christ gave up His spirit. After this reading, a prayer is said and the dismissal is given.

As soon as the dismissal has been given from before the Cross, everyone gathers together in the major church, the Martyrium, and there everything which they have been doing regularly throughout this week from the ninth hour when they came together at the Martyrium, until evening, is then done. After the dismissal from the Martyrium, everyone comes to the Anastasis, and, after they have arrived there, the passage from the Gospel is read where Joseph seeks from Pilate the body of the Lord and places it in a new tomb. After this reading a prayer is said, the catechumens are blessed, and the faithful as well; then the dismissal is given.

On this day no one raises his voice to say the vigil will be continued at the Anastasis, because it is known that the people are tired. However, it is the custom that the vigil be held there. And so, those among the people who wish, or rather those who are able, to keep the vigil, do so until dawn; whereas those who are not able to do so, do not keep watch there. But those of the clergy who are either strong enough or young enough, keep watch there, and hymns and antiphons are sung there all through the night until morning. The greater part of the people keep watch, some from evening on, others from midnight, each one doing what he can.

On the following day, which is Saturday, there is as usual a service at the third hour and again at the sixth hour. There is no service, however, at the ninth hour on Saturday, for preparation is being made for the Easter vigil in the major church, the Martyrium. The Easter vigil is observed here exactly as we observe it at home. Only one thing is done more elaborately here. After the neophytes have been baptized and dressed as soon as they came forth from the baptismal font, they are led first of all to the Anastasis with the bishop. The bishop goes within the railings of the Anastasis, a hymn is sung, and he prays for them. Then he returns with them to the major church, where all the people are holding the vigil as is customary.

Everything is done which is customarily done at home with us, and after the sacrifice has been offered, the dismissal is given. After the vigil service has been celebrated in the major church, everyone comes to the Anastasis singing hymns. There, once again, the text of the Gospel of the Resurrection is read, a prayer is said, and once again the bishop offers the sacrifice. However, for the sake of the people, everything is done rapidly, lest they be delayed too long. And so the people are dismissed. On this day the dismissal from the vigil takes place at the same hour as at home with us.

The eight days of Easter are observed just as at home with us. The liturgy is celebrated in the prescribed manner throughout the eight days of Easter just as it is celebrated everywhere from Easter Sunday to its octave. There is the same decoration, and the same arrangement for these eight days of Easter, as for the Epiphany, both in the major church and in the Anastasis, in the Cross as well as the Eleona, in Bethlehem, and in the Lazarium, too, and indeed everywhere, for this is Easter time.

On that first Sunday, Easter Day, everyone assembles for the liturgy in the major church, in the Martyrium, and on Monday and Tuesday also. But it always happens that, once the dismissal has been given from the Martyrium, everyone comes to the Anastasis singing hymns. On Wednesday everyone assembles for the liturgy in the Eleona; on Thursday, in the Anastasis; on Friday, at Sion; and on Saturday, before the Cross. On Sunday, however, on the octave that is, they go once again to the major church, to the Martyrium. During the eight days of Easter, everyday after lunch, in the company of all the clergy and the neophytes—I mean those who have just been baptized—and all the *aputactitae*, both men and women, and of as many of the people as wish to come, the bishop goes up to the Eleona. Hymns are sung and prayers are said, both in the church which is on the Eleona and where the grotto in which Jesus taught His disciples is located, and at the Imbomon, the place, that is, from which the Lord ascended into heaven. After Psalms have been sung and a prayer has been said, everyone comes down from there, singing hymns, and goes to the Anastasis at the hour for vespers. This is done throughout the eight days.

On Easter Sunday, after the dismissal from vespers at the Anastasis, all the people singing hymns conduct the bishop to Sion. When they have arrived there, hymns proper to the day and the place are sung, and a prayer is said. Then is read the passage from the Gospel describing how on this day and in this very place where there is now this same Church of Sion, the Lord came to His disciples, although the doors were closed, at the time when one of the disciples, namely, Thomas, was not there. When he returned, he said to the other apostles, who had told him that they had seen the Lord: *I will not believe, unless I see.* After this passage has been read, a prayer is again said, the catechumens and then the faithful are blessed, and everyone returns to his home late, around the second hour of the night.

Questions

1. Describe how the Church's prayer during Holy Week involves the imitation of Christ.
2. Describe the different services, devotions, and vigils.
3. What is the role of singing in the prayer of the Church?

St. Gregory of Nyssa

![line]

St. Gregory of Nyssa (335–394) came from an extraordinary family. His father, two brothers, and sister are all venerated as saints. After the death of his wife, St. Gregory entered the monastery founded by his brother, St. Basil the Great, and in his mid-thirties he became bishop of Nyssa. At age forty-six he participated in the Council of Constantinople, where Arianism was decisively condemned thanks in large part to the theological contributions of himself, his brother St. Basil, and their close friend St. Gregory of Nazianzus. These three, known as the "Cappadocian Fathers" because of their ministry in Cappadocia (modern Turkey), remain the most venerated theologians of the Eastern Church. The following selection comes from St. Gregory's treatise on the Lord's Prayer. He emphasizes that we must give prayer the time and energy that it deserves. Prayer provides the intimacy with God that sustains all our other endeavors and that focuses our mind on realities that last.

THE DIVINE WORD TEACHES US THE science of prayer. And to the disciples worthy of it, who eagerly asked to learn to pray in such a way as to win the favour of the Divine hearing, this science is proposed in the

Excerpts from *St. Gregory of Nyssa: The Lord's Prayer, The Beatitudes*, from Ancient Christian Writers, no. 18, edited by Johannes Quasten, S.T.D., and Joseph C. Plumpe, Ph.D., 21–28. Copyright © 1978, The Newman Press, N.Y./Mahwah, N.J. Used with permission of Paulist Press. www.paulistpress.com.

words that prayer should take. Now, I make bold to add a little to what Scripture says; for the present congregation needs instruction not so much on how to pray, as on the necessity of praying at all, a necessity that has perhaps not yet been grasped by most people. In fact, the majority of men grievously neglect in their life this sacred and divine work which is prayer. In this matter, therefore, I think it right first of all to insist as much as possible that one must persevere in prayer, as the Apostle says; secondly, that we must listen attentively to the Divine Voice which proposes to us the manner in which we should offer prayer to the Lord. For I see that in this present life men give their attention to everything else, one concentrating on this matter, another on that; but no one devotes his zeal to the good work of prayer.

The tradesman rises early to attend to his shop, anxious to display his wares sooner than his competitors so as to get in before them, to be the first to attend to the customer and sell his stock. The customer does the same; he takes good care not to miss what he wants by letting someone else anticipate him; and so he hastens not to church but to the market. Thus all are equally keen on gain and anxious to be on the spot before their neighbours, and the hour for prayer is usurped by those things that hold their interest and is turned into time for trafficking.

It is the same with the craftsman, with the orator, with the man who brings a lawsuit as well as with the judge; everyone devotes all his energy to the work he has in hand, forgetting completely the work of prayer because he thinks that the time he gives to God is lost to the work he has purposed to do. For the craftsman considers that the Divine assistance is quite useless for the work he has in hand. Therefore he leaves prayer aside and places all his hopes in his hands, without remembering Him who has given him his hands. In the same way someone who carefully composes a speech does not think of Him who has given him speech; but he pursues his own and his pupils' studies as if he had brought himself into this existence; hence he fails to realize that something good might come to him through the action of God and prefers study to prayer. It is the same with the other occupations: the fact that the mind centers its attention on material, earthly things prevents the soul from devoting itself to the better, heavenly things. Thus it comes about that life is so full of sin, which is always increasing in growth and involved in all human pursuits; therefore everyone keeps forgetting God, and men do not count prayer among the good things worth pursuing. Covetousness enters together with trade; but covetousness is idolatry.

Thus the husbandman does not cultivate the land according to his needs, but is always intent on getting more, and so makes a large entrance for sin in his profession by enlarging his property at the expense of others. Hence arise disputes which are difficult to compose, people becoming incensed against each other over their boundaries, because they are all afflicted with the same disease of covetousness. Hence arise feuds, occasions of evil and attacks on one another that often end in bloodshed and murder. In the same way the contentions in the courts give rise to a variety of sins and find a host of excuses for injustice. The judge, for example, may either willfully incline the balance of justice towards the side of gain, or be involuntarily misled by the subtlety of those who distort the truth, and thus gives an unjust judgment. But how could anyone describe in detail all the different ways in which sin is mixed up with human life? And the reason for this is none other than that men will not ask the help of God for the things they have in hand.

If work is preceded by prayer, sin will find no entrance into the soul. For when the consciousness of God is firmly established in the heart, the devices of the devil remain sterile, and matters of dispute will always be settled according to justice. Prayer prevents the farmer from committing sin, for his fruit will multiply even on a small plot of land, so that sin no longer enters together with the desire for more. It is the same with everyone; with the traveler, with somebody who prepares an expedition or a marriage. Whatever anyone may set out to do, if it is done with prayer the undertaking will prosper and he will be kept from sin, because there is nothing to oppose him and drag the soul into passion. If, on the other hand, a man leaves God out and gives his attention to nothing but his business, then he is inevitably opposed to God, because he is separated from Him. For a person who does not unite himself to God through prayer is separated from God. Therefore we must learn first of all *that we ought always to pray and not to faint.* For the effect of prayer is union with God, and if someone is with God, he is separated from the enemy. Through prayer we guard our chastity, control our temper, and rid ourselves of vanity; it makes us forget injuries, overcomes envy, defeats injustice, and makes amends for sin. Through prayer we obtain physical well-being, a happy home, and a strong, well-ordered society. Prayer will make our nation powerful, will give us victory in war and security in peace; it reconciles enemies and preserves allies. Prayer is the seal of virginity and a pledge of faithfulness in marriage; it shields the wayfarer, protects the sleeper, and gives courage to those who keep vigil. It obtains a good harvest for the farmer and a safe port for the sailor.

Prayer is your advocate in lawsuits. If you are in prison, it will obtain your release; it will refresh you when you are weary and comfort you when you are sorrowful. Prayer is the delight of the joyful as well as solace to the afflicted. It is the wedding crown of the spouses and the festive joy of a birthday no less than the shroud that enwraps us in death.

Prayer is intimacy with God and contemplation of the invisible. It satisfies our yearnings and makes us equal to the angels. Through it good prospers, evil is destroyed, and sinners will be converted. Prayer is the enjoyment of things present and the substance of the things to come. Prayer turned the whale into a home for Jonas; it brought Ezechias back to life from the very gates of death; it transformed the flames into a moist wind for the Three Children. Through prayer the Israelites triumphed over the Amalecites, and 185,000 Assyrians were slain one night by the invisible sword. Past history furnishes thousands of other examples beside these which make it clear that of all the things valued in this life nothing is more precious than prayer. I wish we could already turn to prayer itself; but we would rather add a little to what has been said, and consider how many diverse good things we have received from Divine grace, for the gift of which we should make a return to our Benefactor by prayer and thanksgiving.

Now I think that, even if we spent our whole life in constant communion with God in prayer and thanksgiving, we should be as far from having made Him an adequate return as if we had not even begun to desire making the Giver of all good things such a return.

Time is measured by a threefold division, past, present, and future. In all three we receive the munificence of the Lord. If you consider the present, it is through Him that you live; if the future, your hope that your expectations might be fulfilled is founded on Him; if the past, you will realize that you did not even exist before He made you. Your very birth you have received as a benefit from Him; and once born, another benefit was conferred on you in that, as the Apostle says, you should live and move in Him. The hopes of the future depend upon the same Divine action. You, however, are master only of the present. Therefore, even if you never cease to give thanks to God throughout your life, you will hardly thank Him for the present; and as for the future and the past, you will not be able to find a means of rendering Him His due.

Yet, though we are so far from being able to thank Him properly, we do not even show our good intention as far as we can—I will not say all day long, but not even by devoting a tiny part of the day to the service of God. Who has spread the earth under my feet? Whose wisdom has made water passable? Who has set up the vault of the sky? Who carries the sun before me like a torch? Who causes the springs to come forth from ravines? Who has given the rivers their beds? Who has subjected the animals to my service? Who, when I was but lifeless ashes, gave me both life and a mind? Who fashioned this clay in the image of the Divine? And, when this Divine Image had been tarnished by sin, did not He restore it to its former beauty? When I was exiled from Paradise, deprived of the tree of life, and submerged in the gulf of material things, was it not He who brought me back to man's first beatitude? *There is none that understandeth,* says the Scripture.

Truly, if we considered these things, we should give thanks all our life without ceasing; but actually human nature is almost completely involved in the pursuit of material things. For these it is eagerly ready, with these memory and hope are occupied. In its desire for more, human nature gives itself no rest whatever where there is a chance of gain. Whether it be a question of honour and reputation, of abundant wealth, or of the disease of carnal appetite, in all these things nature desires increase. Yet to the truly good things of God, both those that can already be seen and those that are promised, no thought is given. But it is time to consider as far as we are able the meaning of the words of the prayer.

It is clear that in order to obtain our desires we must learn how we ought to pray. What, then, are we taught about it? *When you are praying, do not babble as the heathens. For they think that in their much speaking they may be heard.* Perhaps the meaning of the teaching is quite clear in itself. It is cast in rather simple language. It needs no subtle learning, except that it is worth discussing what is meant by the term *battalogia* (babbling), so that by realizing its sense we may avoid what is forbidden. It seems to me that He is castigating empty minds and crushing those who immerse themselves in vain desires. Hence He invented this strange novelty of a word in order to rebuke those foolish people who rush hither and thither in order to gratify their desires for completely useless things. For the sensible and rational word, which is concerned with useful things, is properly called a *logos* (word), but that which is poured forth by vain desires for empty pleasures is not a *logos*, but a *battalogia*. And if anyone would explain the meaning in better Greek, he would say *phlyaria* (nonsense) or *leros* (humbug) or *phlenaphos* (chatter), or something like that.

Which advice, therefore, does this passage give us? That in the time of prayer we should not allow such things to enter as passion puts into the mind of fools. For example, childish people do not reflect how a thing could possibly take place according to their fancy, but they imagine for all they are worth wonderful things happening to themselves. They daydream about riches, marriages and kingdoms and big cities that are to be called by their name, and they imagine that they actually are in such a position as their silly ideas suggest.

There are people who are gripped even more violently by this folly. Passing beyond the limits of nature, they develop wings or shine like stars, or carry mountains in their hands; they journey through the heavens or live for myriads of years, becoming young again in their old age, and whatever other bubbles the empty mind of childish people may throw up. Now supposing someone was engaged in some work and did not give his attention to things promising good results, but busied himself with ridiculous aspirations—he would be making a pitiful fool of himself, wasting on these daydreams the time he ought to spend thinking out some profitable proposition. In the same way if a man during prayer is not intent on what profits his soul, but would rather that God should fall in with the emotional uncertainties of his own mind, he is truly like a silly *battalogos*, who prays that God should become a willing servant to his own crazy ideas.

Questions

1. What is a *battalogos*?
2. Why does St. Gregory call for zeal in prayer?
3. For what, according to St. Gregory, are we to pray?

John Cassian

John Cassian, born in 360 in what is now Rumania, died in Marseilles in 435. As a young man, John traveled to Bethlehem and lived in a monastery there. In his twenties, he stayed for seven years among the famous monastic communities in Egypt, which had been inspired by St. Anthony. John Cassian was ordained a deacon in his late thirties by St. John Chrysostom, then bishop of Constantinople, and when Chrysostom was exiled, Cassian traveled to Rome on his behalf. In 415, Cassian founded two monasteries in Marseilles, one for men and one for women. His greatest contribution consists in this bringing of monastic wisdom from the East into the Latin West, and his writings testify to this wisdom. The following selection, cast in the form of a dialogue between the master Isaac and the young monk Germanus, carefully describes four types of Christian prayer and then offers a short commentary on the Lord's Prayer. The selection reveals Cassian's profound knowledge of Scripture.

"WHEN THE SOUL IS SOLIDLY ROOTED in this peacefulness, when it is freed of the bonds of every carnal urge, when the unshaking thrust of the heart is toward the one supreme Good, then the words of

Excerpts from John Cassian, *Conferences*, from The Classics of Western Spirituality, translation and preface by Colm Luibheid, introduction by Owen Chadwick, 106–17. Copyright © 1985 by Colm Luibheid, Paulist Press, Inc., New York/Mahwah, N.J. Used with permission of Paulist Press. www.paulistpress.com.

the apostle will be fulfilled. 'Pray without cease,' he said (1 Thess. 5:17). 'In every place lift up pure hands, with no anger and no rivalry' (1 Tim. 2:8). Sensibility is, so to speak, absorbed by this purity. It is reshaped in the likeness of the spiritual and the angelic so that all its dealings, all its activity will be prayer, utterly pure, utterly without tarnish."

Germanus: "If only we could continue to hold on to those seeds of spiritual thought in the same way and with the same ease as we originate them! They come alive in our hearts as we think back to Scripture, or at the reminder of some spiritual act or as we contemplate some heavenly mysteries, and then, without our knowing it, they very quickly fly away and vanish. No sooner does the mind discover some other opportunities for spiritual thoughts than something else breaks in and what was grasped now slips and glides off. The soul cannot hold still. It is unable to keep its grip on holy thoughts. Even when it seems to have caught on to them, it looks as if its possession of them is the result not of effort but of chance. Indeed, how can the fact that they rise up within us be ascribed to any choice of ours when we actually have no capacity to keep them there within us?

"But I would prefer not to allow the consideration of this matter to take us too far from our theme or to delay what you propose to explain regarding the nature of prayer. It can be looked at in due time. What we wish to ask you now is to tell us about the nature of prayer, and we do so particularly since the blessed apostle warns us never to cease from our prayer. 'Pray without cease' (1 Thess. 5:17).

"First, then, we would like you to tell us about the nature of prayer, about the character it should always have. Then we would like you to tell us how to keep with it in all its forms, how to engage in it without interruption. It cannot be achieved by a poorly stirred heart. We know this from everyday experience and we know it too from those words of your holiness in which you defined the objective of the monk and the highpoint of perfection as 'the consummation of prayer.'"

Isaac: "Apart from great purity of intent and of soul, as well as the illumination of the Holy Spirit, there is nothing, I believe, which can mark off all the forms of prayer from one another. The differences are as great and as numerous as can be encountered within a single soul or, rather, within all souls in all their various conditions and states. I recognize that my own insensitivity makes it impossible for me to perceive them all. Still, to the extent allowed by my own poor experience, I will try to describe them.

"Prayer changes at every moment in proportion to the degree of purity in the soul and in accordance with the extent to which the soul is moved either by outside influence or of itself. Certainly the same kind of prayers cannot be uttered continuously by any one person. A lively person prays one way. A person brought down by the weight of gloom or despair prays another. One prays another way when the life of the spirit is flourishing, and another way when pushed down by the mass of temptation. One prays differently, depending on whether one is seeking the gift of some grace or virtue or the removal of some sinful vice. The prayer is different once again when one is sorrowing at the thought of hell and the fear of future judgment, or when one is fired by hope and longing for future blessedness, when one is in need or peril, in peace or tranquility, when one is flooded with the light of heavenly mysteries or when one is hemmed in by aridity in virtue and staleness in one's thinking.

"So much for the differences within prayer, and they touch all too briefly on a theme of major substance. So much for them, however, since I have so little time in which to discuss them, and in any case the dimness of my own mind and the dullness of my own heart cannot fully take them in. But there is a more serious difficulty here, namely to describe the different types of prayers.

"The apostle notes four types. 'My advice is that first of all supplication should be offered up for everyone, prayers, pleas, and thanksgiving' (1 Tim. 2:1). Now one may be sure that this division was not foolishly made by the apostle. So we must first inquire what is meant by prayer, by petitions, by intercessions, and by thanksgiving. Then we must discover whether all are linked together at the same time in the one supplication, or whether they must be utilized one by one and separately. Should one offer petitions now, prayers some other time, or should one person offer intercessions now, another prayers, another blessings to God—and all this in accordance with the measure of age in which each soul manifests the effort of its zeal.

"The first item to be discussed is the exact meaning of the terms. What is the difference between prayer, supplication, and plea? Then the question must be asked whether these must be utilized one by one or together. And thirdly there is the question of whether the order laid down by the authority of the apostle has something more by way of instruction for the listener. Can the distinction made by the apostle be taken simply as it stands? Did he make it without any further purpose in mind? Actually, this last would seem absurd to me. It is incredible that the Holy Spirit spoke through the apostle something that was transitory and purposeless. Therefore with the Lord's help we will consider these types one by one, in the sequence given above.

" 'My advice is that supplication should be offered up for everyone.' A supplication is a plea or petition made on account of present and past sin by someone who is moved by contrition to seek pardon.

"In prayers we offer or promise something to God. The Greek term means 'vow.' Greek has 'I shall offer my vows to the Lord' and in Latin it is 'I shall do what I have promised to the Lord' (Ps. 117:14), which, according to the sense of the term, may be taken as 'I shall make my prayer to the Lord.' In Ecclesiastes we read: 'If you have made a promise to God do not delay in fulfilling it' (Eccl. 5:3). The Greek has 'If you are to pray to the Lord, do not delay about it.'

"This is how each of us must do this. We pray when we renounce this world, when we undertake to die to all the world's deeds and mode of living and to serve the Lord with all our heart's zeal. We pray when we promise to despise worldly glory and earth's riches and to cling to the Lord with contrite hearts and poverty of spirit. We pray when we promise to put on the purest bodily chastity and unswerving patience or when we vow to drag completely from our hearts the root of anger and the gleam which is the harbinger of death. And if we are brought down by laziness, if we return to our old sinful ways because of not doing at all what we promised, we shall have to answer for our prayers and our commitments and it will be said of us, 'Better not to promise than to promise and not deliver.' As the Greek would have it, 'It is better that you do not pray than that, having prayer, you do not do as you had undertaken' (Eccl. 5:4).

"Third come pleas. We usually make them for others when we ourselves are deeply moved in spirit. We offer them for those dear to us or when we beg for peace in the world or, to borrow the words of the apostle, when we are suppliants 'on behalf of all men, on behalf of rulers and on behalf of all those in high places' (1 Tim. 2:1–2).

"Fourth are thanksgivings. Unspeakably moved by the memory of God's past kindnesses, by the vision of what He now grants or by all that He holds out as a future reward to those who love Him, the mind gives thanks. In this perspective richer prayers are often uttered. Looking with purest gaze at the rewards promised to the saints, our spirit is moved by measureless joy to pour out wordless thanksgiving to God.

"These, then, are the four rich sources of prayer. Out of contrition for sin is supplication born. Prayer comes of the fidelity to promises and the fulfillment of what we have undertaken for the sake of a pure conscience. Pleading comes forth from the warmth of our love. Thanksgiving is generated by the contemplation of God's goodness and greatness and faithfulness. And all this, as we know, often evokes the most fervent and fiery prayers.

"Hence all of these types of prayer of which I have been speaking are valuable for all men, and indeed quite necessary. And so one man will now offer supplication, prayer then, later the purest and most zealous pleas.

"Nevertheless, the first type seems especially appropriate for beginners, for they are still goaded by the stings and by the memory of past sin. The second type is appropriate for those who are making progress in the acquisition of virtue and in the exaltedness of their souls. The third is suitable for those who live as they have promised to do, who see the frailty of others and who speak out for them because of the charity that moves them. The fourth suits those who have pulled the painful thorn of penitence out of their hearts and who in the quiet of their purified spirit contemplate the kindness and mercy that the Lord has shown them in the past, that He gives them now and that He makes ready for them in the future. Aflame with all this their hearts are rapt in the burning prayer which human words can neither grasp nor utter. Sometimes the soul which has come to be rooted in this state of real purity takes on all the forms of prayer at the same time. It flies from one to the other, like an uncontrollable grasping fire. It becomes an outpouring of living pure prayer which the Holy Spirit, without our knowing it, lifts up to God in unspeakable groanings. It conceives so much within itself at that instant, unspeakably pours forth so much in supplication, that it could not tell you of it at another time nor even remember it all.

"It may also happen that one can pray intensely and purely even at the first and lowliest stage when the mind is on the judgment to come. The soul, trembling with fright and fear at the thought of the examination and judgment, is touched at that hour by contrition, and out from its supplication comes an abundance of spiritual fervor so that it is as possessed as that soul which in shining purity contemplates the goodness of God and dissolves in unspeakable joy and happiness. It is all the more loving, as the Lord said, because of all that extra forgiveness which it knows it has received.

"But with an ever more perfect life and by perfect virtue we especially must be carried along toward the types of prayer which are rooted in the contemplation of eternal goodness and in a fervor of love. If I may use humbler language and words more suited to the measure of beginners, we must be carried along toward the forms of prayer which arise out of the wish to acquire a virtue or the urge to kill off a vice. In no way can our spirit attain those more exalted modes of prayer of which I have been speaking except by the step-by-step journey upward through all those pleas we pour forth.

"The Lord Himself deigned to initiate those four types of prayer and He gave us examples of them, so that there was a fulfillment of those words said of Him: 'What Jesus began to do and to teach' (Acts 1:1).

"He offers a supplication when He says: 'Father, if possible, let this chalice pass from me' (Matt. 26:39). And there are the words put in His mouth in the psalm 'My God, my God, look at me. Why have you abandoned me?' (Ps. 21:2). And there are others like this.

"There is a prayer when He says: 'I have glorified you on earth and I have finished the work which you gave me to do' (John 17:4). And this: 'For their sake I consecrate myself so that they may be consecrated in the truth' (John 17:19).

"There is a plea when He says: 'Father, I wish those you have given me to be with me where I am so that they may see the glory which you have given me' (John 17:24). And He certainly makes a plea when He says: 'Father, forgive them for they do not know what they are doing' (Luke 23:24).

"There is blessing when He says: 'I confess to you, Father, Lord of heaven and of earth, for you have hidden these things from the wise and the prudent and have revealed them to the lowly. Yes indeed, Father, for this is what has pleased you' (Matt. 11:25–26). A blessing there surely is when He says: 'Father, I thank you because you have listened to me. Indeed I knew that you always listened to me' (John 11:41–42).

"It is clear to us that these types of prayer can be distinguished and also used at different times. However, the Lord also showed by example that they can all be put together in one perfect prayer, as in that prayer which, as we read at the end of the gospel of John, He poured forth in such abundance. It would take too long to cite the whole text but a careful inquirer can discover for himself that matters are indeed as I have said.

"The apostle in his letter to the Philippians clearly expresses this same idea though he cites the four types of prayer in a somewhat different order. He shows that they must be offered up out of the one burning zeal. This is what he says: 'In your every prayer and supplication let your pleas be included in your blessings to God' (Phil. 4:6). What he wanted in particular to teach us was that in our prayer and supplication blessings should be mingled with our pleas.

"A state of soul more exalted and more elevated will follow upon these types of prayer. It will be shaped by the contemplation of God alone and by the fire of love, and the mind, melted and cast down into this love, speaks freely and respectfully to God, as though to one's own father.

"We must be careful to aspire to this state of soul. This is what the beginning of the Lord's prayer tells us when it says 'Our Father' (Matt. 6:9). With our own voice we proclaim that the God, the Lord of the universe, is our Father and we thereby assert that we have been called out of the state of servitude to adoption as sons.

"To this we add 'who are in heaven' and we do so to mark the fact that the delay we make during this life of ours on earth is a kind of exile keeping us very distant from our Father. In all terror let us hasten out of it and with all longing let us rush toward that domain which we proclaim to be the abode of our Father. May nothing we do make us unworthy of our profession and the dignity of so wonderful an adoption. May nothing deprive us, like degenerate sons, of the heritage of our Father. May nothing cause us to run into His justice and His anger.

"Drawn as we are to the rank and status of sons we will burn with that continuous respectfulness characteristic of good sons. We will think no more of our own advantage. Our zeal will be poured out, all of it, for the sake of our father's glory. We will say 'hallowed be your name,' and we shall bear witness that our longing, our joy, is for the glory of our Father. We shall be imitators of the one who said thus: 'He who talks about himself is looking for his own glory. As for the one who seeks the glory of whoever sent him, he is telling the truth and there is no injustice in him' (John 7:18).

"Paul, the 'vessel of election,' was filled with such a sentiment. He is even prepared to be anathema to Christ so long as his household grows and so long as the salvation of the entire people of Israel adds to the glory of his Father. He is prepared to die for Christ because he knows that no one can die for the one who is Life itself. And, again, he says this: 'We are glad to be weak—provided you are strong' (2 Cor. 13:9).

"There should be no amazement at the fact that Paul is ready to be anathema to Christ for the sake of the glory of Christ, the conversion of his brethren, and the privilege of his people. The prophet Micah was willing to be a liar and to be excluded from the inspiration of the Holy Spirit provided that the Jewish people could escape those sufferings and the disasters of exile foretold by his own prophecies. 'I would wish to be a man without the Spirit and would rather speak a lie' (Mic. 2:11). And there is of course the love of the lawgiver himself who was not unwilling to die alongside his brothers: 'Lord, this people has committed a great sin. I beg you to pardon them their wrongdoing or else strike me out of the book which you have written' (Exod. 32:31–32).

"The words 'hallowed be your name' could well be understood in the sense that God is hallowed by our perfection. In other words, when we say 'hallowed be your name' to Him what we are really saying is 'Father, make us such as to deserve knowledge and understanding of how holy you are, or at least let your holiness shine forth in the spiritual lives we lead.' And this surely happens as men 'see our good works and glorify our Father in heaven' (Matt. 5:16).

"The second request of the very pure soul is to see the coming of the Father's kingdom.

"What this means first of all is that each day Christ should reign among holy men. And this happens when the devil's power has been driven out of our hearts through the expulsion of sinful foulness and when God has begun to reign within us amid the good odors of virtue. With fornication vanquished, chastity rules; with anger overcome, peace is king; with pride under foot, humility is sovereign.

"There is also the promise, definite in regard to its time of fulfillment, made to all the saints, to all the sons of God, the promise that Christ will say to them 'Come, you blessed ones of my Father, take possession of the kingdom prepared for you from the time of the world's creation' (Matt. 25:34). Gazing eagerly toward that set time, the soul is filled with longing and expectation and it says to Him: 'May your kingdom come' (Matt. 6:10). With its own conscience for a witness, the soul knows that it will enter as a partner at the time of the coming of the kingdom. No sinner will dare to say this or to hope for it, for he will have no wish to see the throne of judgment and he will be fully aware that there will be no palm, no reward for his merits, but rather that he will suffer punishment forthwith.

"The third petition of sons is this: 'May your will be done on earth as it is in heaven.' No greater prayer can be offered than that the things of earth should be put on a level with the things of heaven. 'May your will be done on earth as it is in heaven.' What else is this if not a declaration that men should be like angels, that just as the will of God is fulfilled by the angels in heaven so all men on earth should do, not their will, but His.

"The only man capable of offering up this prayer sincerely will be the one who believes that God arranges everything—the seemingly good and the seemingly bad—for our benefit, that the salvation and the well-being of His own people is more of a care and a concern to Him than to ourselves.

"This prayer can also be interpreted certainly in the following way. God wishes for the salvation of all. This is the opinion of the blessed Paul. 'He wishes all men to be saved and to come to the knowledge of the truth' (1 Tim. 2:4). The prophet Isaiah, speaking as the voice of God the Father, says: 'My wish shall be entirely fulfilled' (Isa. 46:10).

"So then as we give voice to 'may your will be done on earth as it is in heaven' we are saying in other words that 'like those in heaven, Father, may those on earth be saved by the knowledge of your name.'

"'Give us this day our supersubstantial bread' (Matt. 6:11). Another evangelist uses the term 'daily' (Luke 11:3).

"The first expression indicates that this bread has a character that is noble and substantial by virtue of which its exalted splendor and holiness surpass all substances and all creatures.

"With 'daily' the evangelist shows that without this bread we cannot live a spiritual life for even a day. When he says 'this day' he shows that the bread must be eaten each day, that it will not be enough to have eaten yesterday unless we eat similarly today. May our daily poverty encourage us to pour forth this prayer at all times, for there is no day on which it is unnecessary for us to eat this bread so as to strengthen the heart of the person within us.

"'Daily' can also be understood as referring to this present life of ours. That is, 'give us this bread while we linger in this present world. We know that in the time to come you will give it to whoever deserves it but we ask that you give it to us today, for he who has not received it in this life will not be able to partake of it in that next life.'

"'And forgive us our debts as we forgive those in debt to us.' Oh, the unspeakable mercy of God! Not only has He handed to us a model of prayer, not only has He given us a discipline which will make us acceptable to Him, not only because of this necessary formula (by which He teaches us always to pray) has He pulled up the roots both of anger and of gloom, but He has also made a way and a route by which those praying to Him may call on Him to exercise a kindly and indulgent judgment over them. He bestows a means to soften the verdict on us. He gives us the means to urge Him to pardon us on account of the example of forgiveness we ourselves offer when we say 'forgive us as we ourselves have forgiven.' Someone, therefore, having forgiven his own debtors, not those of the Lord, will trust in this prayer and will ask pardon for the sins he has committed.

"But there is something which is not so good. Some of us show gentleness and indulgence to wrongs, no matter how great, which have been done to God. If, however, the wrongs no matter how small are done to us, we wreak punishment cruelly and inexorably. Hence anyone who has not forgiven from the bottom of his heart the wrong done by a brother will be condemned, not pardoned, as he says this prayer, since he will be asking for a more severe judgment. 'Forgive me as I have forgiven.' If he is dealt with as he requested, what is in store for him if not that God, following the example he set, is implacably angry and punishes him without mercy? If, then, we wish to be judged mercifully we must show ourselves to be merciful to those who have done us wrong. We shall be forgiven proportionately with the forgiveness we display to those who, whatever their malice, have injured us.

"Many grow fearful at this and when this prayer is uttered by all the people in church they silently skip this part in case it should seem that by their words they are condemning themselves instead of making excuses for themselves. They do not realize that it is with empty subtlety that they are striving, uselessly, to camouflage themselves before the great judge who had wished to give advance notice of how He would exercise judgment to those praying to Him. Precisely because He did not wish us to find Him cruel and inexorable, He made clear the yardstick by which he made judgment. That was that we would judge the brothers who wronged us as we would wish ourselves to be judged by Him, since 'a judgment without mercy awaits the man who has not shown mercy' (James 2:13).

"There follows 'lead us not into temptation,' out of which comes a problem that is not a minor one. If we pray that we be not permitted to be tempted, where will that constancy come from for which we are to be tested? There is the scriptural statement that every man who has not been tested has not been approved of. There is 'Blessed is the man who endures temptation' (James 1:12). So this cannot be the sense of 'lead us not into temptation.' It is not 'do not allow us ever to be tempted' but rather 'do not allow us to be overcome when we are tempted.'

"Job was tempted. But he was not actually led into temptation. He did not ascribe folly to God. He did not take the road of impiety or blasphemy along which the tempter wished to drag him.

"Abraham was tempted. Joseph was tempted. But neither was led into temptation, for neither of them yielded to the tempter.

"And then there follows 'but deliver us from evil,' that is, 'do not allow us to be tempted beyond endurance by the devil and ensure that "with every temptation there is a way out, so that we can put up with it"' (1 Cor. 10:13).

"You see then the brief mode and formula of prayer given us by the judge to whom our pleas must be offered. There is no request for riches, no reminder of honors, no plea for power or bravery, no reference to bodily well-being or to this present life. The Creator of eternity does not wish that something perishable, something cheap, something time-bound, is sought from Him. It would be a terrible wrong to His generosity and lavishness to ignore requests for what eternally endures in favor of petitions for what is transitory and perishable. This kind of spiritual poverty in our prayers would incur the wrath instead of the favor of our judge.

"It would seem, then, that this prayer, the Our Father, contains the fullness of perfection. It was the Lord Himself who gave it to us as both an example and a rule. It raises up those making use of it to that preeminent situation of which I spoke earlier. It lifts them up to that prayer of fire known to so few. It lifts them up, rather, to that ineffable prayer which rises above all human consciousness, with no voice sounding, no tongue moving, no words uttered. The soul lights up with heavenly illumination and no longer employs constricted, human speech. All sensibility is gathered together and, as though from some very abundant source, the soul breaks forth richly, bursts out unspeakably to God, and in the tiniest instant it pours out so much more than the soul can either describe or remember when it returns again to itself.

"Our Lord, with this formula of pleading, passed through this same condition or situation. He withdrew to the solitude of the mountain, and in the silent prayer of His agony He gave with His bloody sweat an inimitable example of ardor.

"Who could have the experience to describe the different varieties, the causes and the sources of the compunction by means of which the soul is inflamed and is lifted like a fire to the purest and the most fervent prayer? But by way of example and to the best of my ability I will say something about this and cast my mind back, with the Lord's help to guide me.

"Once while I was singing the psalms a verse of it put me in the way of the prayer of fire. Or sometimes the musical expression of a brother's voice has moved sluggish minds to the most intense prayer. I have known it to happen that the superiority and the seriousness of someone giving voice to the psalms has stirred a great onset of zeal in those who were merely bystanders. Sometimes the encouragement and the spiritual discourse of a perfect man have stirred to the richest prayers the sensibilities of those who were depressed. And I know that in my own case the death of a brother or of a friend has moved me to the fullest compunction. The memory too of my lack of warmth and of my carelessness has produced a saving ardor of soul within me.

"In this way, then, there are certainly countless opportunities when, with God's grace, the torpor and the sluggishness of our souls are shaken up."

Questions

1. What are the four types of prayer?
2. What are the four rich sources of prayer?
3. To what state of soul must we aspire?

St. Augustine

The greatest of the Latin Church Fathers, St. Augustine (354–430) was born in North Africa. After teaching in Rome and Milan, where he was baptized by St. Ambrose, he returned to North Africa and served for the remainder of his life as bishop of Hippo. Among St. Augustine's voluminous writings is his commentary on Christ's Sermon on the Mount. The following selection from that work begins with his exposition of Christ's teaching his disciples to pray and includes his commentary on the Lord's Prayer. In learning how to pray, Augustine suggests, we learn how to live.

"AND WHEN YOU PRAY," SAYS HE [Jesus], "you shall not be as the hypocrites are; for they love to pray standing in the synagogues and in the corners of the streets, that they may be seen of men." And here also it is not the being seen of men that is wrong, but doing these things for the purpose of being seen of men; and it is superfluous to make the same remark so often, since there is just one rule to be kept, from which we learn that what we should dread and avoid is not that men know these things, but that they be done with this intent, that the fruit of pleasing men should be sought after in them. Our Lord Himself, too,

From *Our Lord's Sermon on the Mount*, trans. William Findlay and D. S. Schaff, in *Nicene and Post-Nicene Fathers*, vol. 6: *Augustine: Sermon on the Mount, Harmony of the Gospels, Homilies on the Gospels* (Peabody, Mass.: Hendrickson, 1995 [1888]), 37–45.

preserves the same words, when He adds similarly, "Verily I say unto you, They have received their reward"; hereby showing that He forbids this—the striving after that reward in which fools delight when they are praised by men.

"But when you pray," says He, "enter into your bed-chambers." What are those bed-chambers but just our hearts themselves, as is meant also in the Psalm, when it is said, "What you say in your hearts, have remorse for even in your beds"? "And when you have shut the doors," says He, "pray to your Father who is in secret." It is a small matter to enter into our bed-chambers if the door stand open to the unmannerly, through which the things that are outside profanely rush in and assail our inner man. Now we have said that outside are all temporal and visible things, which make their way through the door, *i.e.*, through the fleshly sense into our thoughts, and clamorously interrupt those who are praying by a crowd of vain phantoms. Hence the door is to be shut, *i.e.*, the fleshly sense is to be resisted, so that spiritual prayer may be directed to the Father, which is done in the inmost heart, where prayer is offered to the Father which is in secret. "And your Father," says He, "who seeth in secret, shall reward you." And this had to be wound up with a closing statement of such a kind; for here at the present stage the admonition is not that we should pray, but as to how we should pray. Nor is what goes before an admonition that we should give alms, but as to the spirit in which we should do so, inasmuch as He is giving instructions with regard to the cleansing of the heart, which nothing cleanses but the undivided and single-minded striving after eternal life from the pure love of wisdom alone.

"But when you pray," says He, "do not speak much, as the heathen do; for they think that they shall be heard for their much speaking." As it is characteristic of the hypocrites to exhibit themselves to be gazed at when praying, and their fruit is to please men, so it is characteristic of the heathen, *i.e.*, of the Gentiles, to think they are heard for their much speaking. And in reality, every kind of much speaking comes from the Gentiles, who make it their endeavour to exercise the tongue rather than to cleanse the heart. And this kind of useless exertion they endeavour to transfer even to the influencing of God by prayer, supposing that the Judge, just like man, is brought over by words to a certain way of thinking. "Be not you, therefore, like unto them," says the only true Master. "For your Father knoweth what things are necessary for you, before you ask Him." For if many words are made use of with the intent that one who is ignorant may be instructed and taught, what need is there of them for Him who knows all things, to whom all things which exist, by the very fact of their existence, speak, and show themselves as having been brought into existence; and those things which are future do not remain concealed from His knowledge and wisdom, in which both those things which are past, and those things which will yet come to pass, are all present and cannot pass away?

But since, however few they may be, yet there are words which He Himself also is about to speak, by which He would teach us to pray; it may be asked why even these few words are necessary for Him who knows all things before they take place, and is acquainted, as has been said, with what is necessary for us before we ask Him? Here, in the first place, the answer is, that we ought to urge our case with God, in order to obtain what we wish, not by words, but by the ideas which we cherish in our mind, and by the direction of our thought, with pure love and sincere desire; but that our Lord has taught us the very ideas in words, that by committing them to memory we may recollect those ideas at the time we pray.

But again, it may be asked (whether we are to pray in ideas or in words) what need there is for prayer itself, if God already knows what is necessary for us; unless it be that the very effort involved in prayer calms and purifies our heart, and makes it more capacious for receiving the divine gifts, which are poured into us spiritually. For it is not on account of the urgency of our prayers that God hears us, who is always ready to give us His light, not of a material kind, but that which is intellectual and spiritual: but we are not always ready to receive, since we are inclined towards other things, and are involved in darkness through our desire for temporal things. Hence there is brought about in prayer a turning of the heart to Him, who is ever ready to give, if we will but take what He has given; and in the very act of turning there is effected a purging of the inner eye, inasmuch as those things of a temporal kind which were desired are excluded, so that the vision of the pure heart may be able to bear the pure light, divinely shining, without any setting or change: and not only to bear it, but also to remain in it; not merely without annoyance, but also with ineffable joy, in which a life truly and sincerely blessed is perfected.

But now we have to consider what things we are taught to pray for by Him through whom we both learn what we are to pray for, and obtain what we pray for. "After this manner, therefore, pray you," says He: "Our Father who art in heaven, Hallowed be Thy name. Thy kingdom come. Thy will be done on earth, as it is in heaven. Give us this day our daily bread. And forgive us our debts, as we forgive our debtors. And bring us not into temptation, but deliver us from evil." Seeing that in all prayer we have to conciliate the goodwill of him to whom we pray, then to say what we pray for; goodwill is usually conciliated by our offering praise to him to whom the prayer is directed, and this is usually put in the beginning of the prayer: and in this particular our Lord has bidden us say nothing else but "Our Farther who art in heaven." For many things are said in praise of God, which, being scattered variously and widely over all the Holy Scriptures, every one will be able to consider when he reads them: yet nowhere is there found a precept for the people of Israel, that they should say "Our Father," or that they should pray to God as a Father; but as Lord He was made known to them, as being yet servants, *i.e.*, still living according to the flesh. I say this, however, inasmuch as they received the commands of the law, which they were ordered to observe: for the prophets often show that this same Lord of ours might have been their Father also, if they had not strayed from His commandments: as, for instance, we have that statement, "I have nourished and brought up children, and they have rebelled against me"; and that other, "I have said, You are gods; and all of you are children of the Most High"; and this again, "If then I be a Father, where is my honour? and if I be a Master, where is my fear?" and very many other statements, where the Jews are accused of showing by their sin that they did not wish to become sons: those things being left out of account which are said in prophecy of a future Christian people, that they would have God as a Father, according to that gospel statement, "To them gave He power to become the sons of God." The Apostle Paul, again, says, "The heir, as long as he is a child, differs nothing from a servant"; and mentions that we have received the Spirit of adoption, "whereby we cry, Abba, Father."

And since the fact that we are called to an eternal inheritance, that we might be fellow-heirs with Christ and attain to the adoption of sons, is not of our deserts, but of God's grace; we put this very same grace in the beginning of our prayer, when we say "Our Father." And by that appellation both love is stirred up—for what ought to be dearer to sons than a father?—and a suppliant disposition, when men say to God, "Our Father": and a certain presumption of obtaining what we are about to ask;

since, before we ask anything, we have received so great a gift as to be allowed to call God "Our Father." For what would He not now give to sons when they ask, when He has already granted this very thing, namely, that they might be sons? Lastly, how great solicitude takes hold of the mind, that he who says "Our Father," should not prove unworthy of so great a Father! For if any plebeian should be permitted by the party himself to call a senator of more advanced age father; without doubt he would tremble, and would not readily venture to do it, reflecting on the humbleness of his origin, and the scantiness of his resources, and the worthlessness of his plebeian person: how much more, therefore, ought we to tremble to call God Father, if there is so great a stain and so much baseness in our character, that God might much more justly drive forth these from contact with Himself, than that senator might the poverty of any beggar whatever! Since, indeed, he (the senator) despises that in the beggar to which even he himself may be reduced by the vicissitude of human affairs: but God never falls into baseness of character. And thanks be to the mercy of Him who requires this of us, that He should be our Father—a relationship which can be brought about by no expenditure of ours, but solely by God's goodwill. Here also there is an admonition to the rich and to those of noble birth, so far as this world is concerned, that when they have become Christians they should not comport themselves proudly towards the poor and the low of birth; since together with them they call God "Our Father"—an expression which they cannot truly and piously use, unless they recognize that they themselves are brethren.

Let the new people, therefore, who are called to an eternal inheritance, use the word of the New Testament, and say, "Our Father who art in heaven," *i.e.*, in the holy and the just. For God is not contained in space. For the heavens are indeed the higher material bodies of the world, but yet material, and therefore cannot exist except in some definite place; but if God's place is believed to be in the heavens, as meaning the higher parts of the world, the birds are of greater value than we, for their life is nearer to God. But it is not written, The Lord is nigh unto tall men, or unto those who dwell on mountains; but it is written, "The Lord is nigh unto them that are of a broken heart," which refers rather to humility. But as a sinner is called earth, when it is said to him, "Earth you are, and unto earth shall you return"; so, on the other hand, a righteous man may be called heaven. For it is said to the righteous, "For the temple of God is holy, which temple you are." And therefore, if God dwells in His temple, and the saints are His temple, the expression "who art in heaven" is rightly used in the sense, who art in the saints. And most suitable is such a similitude, so that spiritually there may be seen to be as great a difference between the righteous and sinners, as there is material between heaven and earth.

And for the purpose of showing this, when we stand at prayer, we turn to the east, whence the heaven rises: not as if God also were dwelling there, in the sense that He who is everywhere present, not as occupying space, but by the power of His majesty, had forsaken the other parts of the world; but in order that the mind may be admonished to turn to a more excellent nature, *i.e.,* to God, when its own body, which is earthly, is turned to a more excellent body, *i.e.,* to a heavenly one. It is also suitable for the different stages of religion, and expedient in the highest degree, that in the minds of all, both small and great, there should be cherished worthy conceptions of God. And therefore, as regards those who as yet are taken up with the beauties that are seen, and cannot think of anything incorporeal, inasmuch as they must necessarily prefer heaven to earth, their opinion is more tolerable, if they believe God, whom as yet they think of after a corporeal fashion, to be in heaven rather than upon earth: so that when at any future time they have learned that the dignity of the soul exceeds even a celestial body, they may seek Him in the soul rather than in a celestial body even; and when they have learned how great a distance there is between the souls of sinners and of the righteous, just as they did not venture, when as yet they were wise only after a carnal fashion, to place Him on earth, but in heaven, so afterwards with better faith or intelligence they may seek Him again in the souls of the righteous rather than in those of sinners. Hence, when it is said, "Our Father which art in heaven," it is rightly understood to mean in the hearts of the righteous, as it were in His holy temple. And at the same time, in such a way that he who prays wishes Him whom he invokes to dwell in himself also; and when he strives after this, practices righteousness—a kind of service by which God is attracted to dwell in the soul.

Let us see now what things are to be prayed for. For it has been stated who it is that is prayed to, and where He dwells. First of all, then, of those things which are prayed for comes this petition, "Hallowed be Thy name." And this is prayed for, not as if the name of God were not holy already, but that it may be held holy by men; *i.e.*, that God may so become known to them, that they shall reckon nothing more holy, and which they are more afraid of offending. For, because it is said, "In Judah is God known; His name is great in Israel," we are not to understand the statement in this way, as if God were less in one place, greater in another; but there His name is great, where He is named according to the greatness of his majesty. And so there His name is said to be holy, where He is named with veneration and the fear of offending Him. And this is what is now going on, while the gospel, by becoming known everywhere throughout the different nations, commends the name of the one God by means of the administration of His Son.

In the next place there follows, "Thy kingdom come." Just as the Lord Himself teaches in the Gospel that the day of judgment will take place at the very time when the gospel shall have been preached among all nations: a thing which belongs to the hallowing of God's name. For here also the expression "Thy kingdom come" is not used in such a way as if God were not now reigning. But some one perhaps might say the expression "come" meant *upon earth*; as if, indeed, He were not even now really reigning upon earth, and had not always reigned upon it from the foundation of the world. "Come," therefore, is to be understood in the sense of "manifested to men." For in the same way also as a light which is present is absent to the blind, and to those who shut their eyes; so the kingdom of God, though it never departs from the earth, is yet absent to those who are ignorant of it. But no one will be allowed to be ignorant of the kingdom of God, when His Only-begotten shall come from heaven, not only in a way to be apprehended by the understanding, but also visibly in the person of the Divine Man, in order to judge the quick and the dead. And after that judgment, *i.e.*, when the process of distinguishing and separating the righteous from the unrighteous has taken place, God will so dwell in the righteous, that there will be no need for any one being taught by man, but all will be, as it is written, "taught of God." Then will the blessed life in all its parts be perfected in the saints unto eternity, just as now the most holy and blessed heavenly angels are wise and blessed, from the fact that God alone is their light; because the Lord hath promised this also to His own: "In the resurrection," says He, "they will be as the angels in heaven."

And therefore, after that petition where we say, "Thy kingdom come," there follows, "Thy will be done, as in heaven so in earth": *i.e.*, just as Thy will is in the angels who are in heaven, so that they wholly cleave to Thee, and thoroughly enjoy Thee, no error beclouding their wisdom, no misery hindering their blessedness; so let it be done in Thy saints who are on earth, and made from the earth, so far as the body is concerned, and who, although it is into a heavenly habitation and exchange, are yet to be taken from the earth. To this there is a reference also in that doxology of the angels, "Glory to God in the highest, and on earth peace to men of goodwill: so that when our goodwill has gone before, which follows Him who calls, the will of God is perfected in us, as it is in the heavenly angels; so that no antagonism stands in the way of our blessedness: and this is peace. "Thy will be done" is also rightly understood in the sense of, Let obedience be rendered to Thy precepts: "as in heaven so on earth," *i.e.* as by the angels so by men. For, that the will of God is done when His precepts are obeyed, the Lord Himself says, when He affirms, "My meat is to do the will of Him that sent me"; and often, "I came, not to do my own will, but the will of Him that sent me"; and when He says, "Behold my mother and my brethren! For whosoever shall do the will of God, the same is my brother, and sister, and mother." And therefore, in those at least who do the will of God, the will of God is accomplished; not because they cause God to will, but because they do what He wills, *i.e.* they do according to His will.

There is also that other interpretation, "Thy will be done as in heaven so on earth"—as in the holy and just, so also in sinners. And this, besides, may be understood in two ways: either that we should pray even for our enemies (for what else are they to be reckoned, in spite of whose will the Christian and Catholic name still spreads?), so that it is said, "Thy will be done as in heaven so on earth"—as if the meaning were, As the righteous do Thy will, in like manner let sinners also do it, so that they may be converted unto Thee; or in this sense, "Let Thy will be done as in heaven so on earth," so that every one may get his own; which will take place at the last judgment, the righteous being requited with a reward, sinners with condemnation—when the sheep shall be separated.

That other interpretation also is not absurd, nay, it is thoroughly accordant with both our faith and hope, that we are to take heaven and earth in the sense of spirit and flesh. And since the apostle says, "With the mind I myself serve the law of God, but with the flesh the law of sin," we see that the will of God is done in the mind, *i.e.* in the spirit. But when death shall have been swallowed up in victory, and this mortal shall have put on immortality, which will happen at the resurrection of the flesh, and at that change which is promised to the righteous, according to the prediction of the same apostle, let the will of God be done on earth, as it is in heaven; *i.e.*, in such a way that, in like manner as the spirit does not resist God, but follows and does His will, so the body also may not resist the spirit or soul, which at present is harassed by the weakness of the body, and is prone to fleshly habit: and this will be an element of the perfect peace in the life eternal, that not only will the will be present with us, but also the performance of that which is good. "For to will," says he, "is present with me; but how to perform that which is good I find not": for not yet in earth as in heaven, *i.e.* not yet in the flesh as in the spirit, is the will of God done. For even in our misery the will of God is done, when we suffer those things through the flesh which are due to us in virtue of our mortality, which our nature has deserved because of its sin. But we are to pray for this, that the will of God may be done as in heaven so in earth; that in like manner as with the heart we delight in the law after the inward man, so also, when the change in our body has taken place, no part of us may, on account of earthly griefs or pleasures, stand opposed to this our delight.

Nor is that view inconsistent with truth, that we are to understand the words, "Thy will be done as in heaven so in earth," as in our Lord Jesus Christ Himself, so also in the Church: as if one were to say, As in the man who fulfilled the will of the Father, so also in the woman who is betrothed to him. For heaven and earth are suitably understood as if they were man and wife; since the earth is fruitful from the heaven fertilizing it.

The fourth petition is, "Give us this day our daily bread." Daily bread is put either for all those things which meet the wants of this life, in reference to which He says in His teaching, "Take no thought for the morrow": so that on this account there is added, "Give us this day": or, it is put for the sacrament of the body of Christ, which we daily receive: or, for the spiritual food, of which the same Lord says, "Labour for the meat which perishes not"; and again, "I am the bread of life, which came down from heaven." But which of these three views is the more probable, is a question for consideration. For perhaps some one may obtain the things which are necessary for this life—such, for instance, as food and clothing—when the Lord Himself says, "Be not anxious what you shall eat, or what you shall put on." Can any one not be anxious for a thing which he prays that he may obtain; when prayer is to be offered with so great earnestness of mind, that to this refers all that has been said about shutting our closets, and also the command, "Seek you first the kingdom of God, and His righteousness; and all these things shall be added unto you"? Certainly He does not say, Seek you first the kingdom of God, and then seek those other things; but "all these things," says He, "shall be added unto you," that is to say, even though you are not seeking them. But I know not whether it can be found out, how one is rightly said not to seek what he most earnestly pleads with God that he may receive.

But with respect to the sacrament of the Lord's body (in order that they may not start a question, who, the most of them being in Eastern parts, do not partake of the Lord's supper daily, while this bread is called daily bread: in order, therefore, that they may be silent, and not defend their way of thinking about this matter even by the very authority of the Church, because they do such things without scandal, and are not prevented from doing them by those who preside over their churches, and when they do not obey are not condemned; whence it is proved that this is not understood as daily bread in these parts: for, if this were the case, they would be charged with the commission of a great sin, who do not on that account receive it daily; but, as has been said, not to argue at all to any extent from the case of such parties), this consideration at least ought to occur to those who reflect, that we have received a rule for prayer from the Lord, which we ought not to transgress, either by adding or omitting anything. And since this is the case, who is there who would venture to say that we ought only once to use the Lord's Prayer, or at least that, even if we have used it a second or a third time before the hour at which we partake of the Lord's body, afterwards we are assuredly not so to pray during the remaining hours of the day? For we shall no longer be able to say, "Give us this day," respecting what we have already received; or every one will be able to compel us to celebrate that sacrament at the very last hour of the day.

It remains, therefore, that we should understand the daily bread as spiritual, that is to say, divine precepts, which we ought daily to meditate and to labour after. For just with respect to these the Lord says, "Labour for the meat which perishes not." That food, moreover, is called daily food at present, so long as this temporal life is measured off by means of days that depart and return. And, in truth, so long as the desire of the soul is directed by turns, now to what is higher, now to what is lower, *i.e.* now to spiritual things, now to carnal, as is the case with him who at one time is nourished with food, at another time suffers hunger; bread is daily necessary, in order that the hungry man may be recruited, and he who is falling down may be raised up. As, therefore, our body in this life, that is to say, before that great change, is recruited with food, because it feels loss; so may the soul also, since by means of temporal desires it sustains as it were a loss in its striving after God, be reinvigorated by the food of the precepts. Moreover, it is said, "Give us this day," as long as it is called today, *i.e.,* in this temporal life. For we shall be so abundantly provided with spiritual food after this life unto eternity, that it will not then be called daily bread; because there the flight of time, which causes days to succeed days, whence it may be called to-day, will not exist. But as it is said, "Today, if you will hear His voice," which the apostle interprets in the Epistle to the Hebrews, As long as it is called today; so here also the expression is to be understood, "Give us this day." But if any one wishes to understand the sentence before us also of food necessary for the body, or of the sacrament of the Lord's body, we must take all three meanings conjointly; that is to say, that we are to ask for all at once as daily bread, both the bread necessary for the body, and the visible hallowed bread, and the invisible bread of the word of God.

The fifth petition follows: "And forgive us our debts, as we also forgive our debtors." It is manifest that by debts are meant sins, either from that statement which the Lord Himself makes, "You shalt by no means come out thence, till you have paid the uttermost farthing"; or from the fact that He called those men debtors who were reported to Him as having been killed, either those on whom the tower fell, or those whose blood Herod had mingled with the sacrifice. For He said that men supposed it was because they were debtors above measure, *i.e.,* sinners, and added, "I tell you, Nay: but, except you repent, you shall all likewise die." Here, therefore, it is not a money claim that one is pressed to remit, but whatever sins another may have committed against him.

For we are enjoined to remit a money claim by that precept rather which has been given above, "If any man will sue you at the law, and take away your coat, let him have your cloak also"; nor is it necessary to remit a debt to every money debtor, but only to him who is unwilling to pay, to such an extent that he wishes even to go to law. "Now the servant of the Lord," as says the apostle, "must not go to law." And therefore to him who shall be unwilling, either spontaneously or when requested, to pay the money which he owes, it is to be remitted. For his unwillingness to pay will arise from one of two causes, either that he has it not, or that he is avaricious and covetous of the property of another; and both of these belong to a state of poverty: for the former is poverty of substance, the latter poverty of disposition. Whoever, therefore, remits a debt to such a one, remits it to one who is poor, and performs a Christian work; while that rule remains in force, that he should be prepared in mind to lose what is owing to him. For if he has used exertion in every way, quietly and gently, to have it restored to him, not so much aiming at a money profit, as that he may bring the man round to what is right, to whom without doubt it is hurtful to have the means of paying, and yet not to pay; not only will he not sin, but he will even do a very great service, in trying to prevent that other, who is wishing to make gain of another's money, from making shipwreck of the faith; which is so much more serious a thing, that there is no comparison. And hence it is understood that in this fifth petition also, where we say, "Forgive us our debts," the words are spoken not indeed in reference to money, but in reference to all ways in which any one sins against us, and by consequence in reference to money also. For the man who refuses to pay you the money which he owes, when he has the means of doing so, sins against you. And if you do not forgive this sin, you will not be able to say, "Forgive us, as we also forgive"; but if you pardon it, you see how he who is enjoined to offer such a prayer is admonished also with respect to forgiving a money debt.

That may indeed be construed in this way, that when we say, "Forgive us our debts, as we also forgive," when only are we convicted of having acted contrary to this rule, if we do not forgive them who ask pardon, because we also wish to be forgiven by our most gracious Father when we ask His pardon. But, on the other hand, by that precept whereby we are enjoined to pray for our enemies, it is not for those who ask pardon that we are enjoined to pray. For those who are already in such a state of mind are no longer enemies. By no possibility, however, could one truthfully say that he prays for one whom he has not pardoned. And therefore we must confess that all sins which are committed against us are to be forgiven, if we wish those to be forgiven by our Father which we commit against Him. For the subject of revenge has been sufficiently discussed already, as I think.

The sixth petition is, "And bring us not into temptation." Some manuscripts have the word "lead," which is, I judge, equivalent in meaning: for both translations have arisen from the one Greek word which is used. But many parties in prayer express themselves thus, "Suffer us not to be led into temptation"; that is to say, explaining in what sense the word "lead" is used. For God does not Himself lead, but suffers that man to be led into temptation whom He has deprived of His assistance, in accordance with a most hidden arrangement, and with his deserts. Often, also, for manifest reasons, He judges him worthy of being so deprived, and allowed to be led into temptation. But it is one thing to be led into temptation, another to be tempted. For without temptation no one can be proved, whether to himself, as it is written, "He who has not been tempted, what manner of things does he know?" or to another, as the apostle says, "And your temptation in my flesh you despised not": For from this circumstance he learnt that they were steadfast, because they were not turned aside from charity by those tribulations which had happened to the apostle according to the flesh. For even before all temptations we are known to God, who knows all things before they happen.

When, therefore, it is said, "The Lord your God tempts (proves) you, that He may know if you love Him," the words "that He may know" are employed for what is the real state of the case, that He may make you know: just as we speak of a joyful day, because it makes us joyful; of a sluggish frost, because it makes us sluggish; and of innumerable things of the same sort, which are found either in ordinary speech, or in the discourse of learned men, or in the Holy Scriptures. And the heretics who are opposed to the Old Testament, not understanding this, think that the brand of ignorance, as it were, is to be placed upon Him of whom it is said, "The Lord your God tempts you": as if in the Gospel it were not written of the Lord, "And this He said to tempt (prove) him, for He Himself knew what He would do." For if He knew the heart of him whom He was tempting, what is it that He wished to see by tempting him? But in reality, that was done in order that he who was tempted might become known to himself, and that he might condemn his own despair, on the multitudes being filled with the Lord's bread, while he had thought they had not enough to eat.

Here, therefore, the prayer is not, that we should not be tempted, but that we should not be brought into temptation: as if, were it necessary that any one should be examined by fire, he should pray, not that he should not be touched by the fire, but that he should not be consumed. For "the furnace proves the potter's vessels, and the trial of tribulation righteous men." Joseph therefore was tempted with the allurement of debauchery, but he was not brought into temptation. Susanna was tempted, but she was not led or brought into temptation; and many others of both sexes: but Job most of all, in regard to whose admirable steadfastness in the Lord his God, those heretical enemies of the Old Testament, when they wish to mock at it with sacrilegious mouth, brandish this above other weapons, that Satan begged that he should be tempted. For they put the question to unskillful men by no means able to understand such things, how Satan could speak with God: not understanding (for they cannot, inasmuch as they are blinded by superstition and controversy) that God does not occupy space by the mass of His corporeity; and thus exist in one place, and not in another, or at least have one part here, and another elsewhere: but that He is everywhere present in His majesty, not divided by parts, but everywhere complete. But if they take a fleshly view of what is said, "the heaven is my throne, and the earth is my footstool"—to which passage our Lord also bears testimony, when He says, "Swear not at all: neither by heaven, for it is God's throne; nor by the earth, for it is His footstool"—what wonder if the devil, being placed on earth, stood before the feet of God, and spoke something in His presence? For when will they be able to understand that there is no soul, however wicked, which can yet reason in any way, in whose conscience God does not speak? For who but God has written the law of nature in the hearts of men?—that law concerning which the apostle says: "For when the Gentiles, who have not the law, do by nature the things contained in the law, these, having not the law, are a law unto themselves: which show the work of the law written in their hearts, their conscience also bearing them witness, and their thoughts the meanwhile accusing or else excusing one another, in the day when the Lord shall judge the secrets of men." And therefore, as in the case of every rational soul, which thinks and reasons, even though blinded by passion, we attribute whatever in its reasoning is true, not to itself but to the very light of truth by which, however faintly, it is according to its capacity illuminated, so as to perceive some measure of truth by its reasoning; what wonder if the depraved spirit of the devil, perverted though it be by lust, should be represented as having heard from the voice of God Himself, *i.e.* from the voice of the very Truth, whatever true thought it has entertained about a righteous man whom it was proposing to tempt? But whatever is false is to be attributed to that lust from which he has received the name of devil. Although it is also the case that God has often spoken by means of a corporeal and visible creature whether to good or bad, as being Lord and Governor of all, and Disposer according to the merits of every deed: as, for instance, by means of angels, who appeared also under the aspect of men; and by means of the prophets, saying, Thus saith the Lord. What wonder then, if, though not in mere thought, at least by means of some creature fitted for such a work, God is said to have spoken with the devil?

And let them not imagine it unworthy of His dignity, and as it were of His righteousness, that God spoke with him: inasmuch as He spoke with an angelic spirit, although one foolish and lustful, just as if He were speaking with a foolish and lustful human spirit. Or let such parties themselves tell us how He spoke with that rich man, whose most foolish covetousness He wished to censure, saying: "You fool, this night your soul shall be required of you: then whose shall those things be which you have provided?" Certainly the Lord Himself says so in the Gospel, to which those heretics, whether they will or no, bend their necks. But if they are puzzled by this circumstance, that Satan asks from God that a righteous man should be tempted; I do not explain how it happened, but I compel them to explain why it is said in the Gospel by the Lord Himself to the disciples, "Behold, Satan hath desired to have you, that he may sift you as wheat"; and He says to Peter, "But I have prayed for you, that your faith fail not." And when they explain this to me, they explain to themselves at the same time that which they question me about. But if they should not be able to explain this, let them not dare with rashness to blame in any book what they read in the Gospel without offence.

Temptations, therefore, take place by means of Satan not by his power, but by the Lord's permission, either for the purpose of punishing men for their sins, or of proving and exercising them in accordance with the Lord's compassion. And there is a very great difference in the nature of the temptations into which each one may fall. For Judas, who sold his Lord, did not fall into one of the same nature as Peter fell into, when, under the influence of terror, he denied his Lord. There are also temptations common to man, I believe, when every one, though well disposed, yet yielding to human frailty, falls into error in some plan, or is irritated against a brother, in the earnest endeavour to bring him round to what is right, yet a little more than Christian calmness demands: concerning which temptations the apostle says, "There hath no temptation taken you but such as is common to man"; while he says at the same time, "But

God is faithful, who will not suffer you to be tempted above that you are able; but will with the temptation also make a way to escape, that you may be able to bear it." And in that sentence he makes it sufficiently evident that we are not to pray that we may not be tempted, but that we may not be led into temptation. For we are led into temptation, if such temptations have happened to us as we are not able to bear. But when dangerous temptations, into which it is ruinous for us to be brought and led, arise either from prosperous or adverse temporal circumstances, no one is broken down by the irksomeness of adversity, who is not led captive by the delight of prosperity.

The seventh and last petition is, "But deliver us from evil." For we are to pray not only that we may not be led into the evil from which we are free, which is asked in the sixth place; but that we may also be delivered from that into which we have been already led. And when this has been done, nothing will remain terrible, nor will any temptation at all have to be feared. And yet in this life, so long as we carry about our present mortality, into which we were led by the persuasion of the serpent, it is not to be hoped that this can be the case; but yet we are to hope that at some future time it will take place: and this is the hope which is not seen, of which the apostle, when speaking, said, "But hope which is seen is not hope." But yet the wisdom which is granted in this life also, is not to be despaired of by the faithful servants of God. And it is this, that we should with the most wary vigilance shun what we have understood, from the Lord's revealing it, is to be shunned; and that we should with the most ardent love seek after what we have understood, from the Lord's revealing it, is to be sought after. For thus, after the remaining burden of this mortality has been laid down in the act of dying, there shall be perfected in every part of man at the fit time, the blessedness which has been begun in this life, and which we have from time to time strained every nerve to lay hold of and secure.

Questions

1. What, according to St. Augustine, is our "daily bread"?
2. How does St. Augustine explain temptations?
3. Describe how St. Augustine connects the words "Our Father" with grace.

St. Thomas Aquinas

Born into a noble family and raised in the famous Benedictine monastery of Monte Cassino, where his family intended him to be abbot, St. Thomas Aquinas (1225–1274) instead joined the fledgling Dominican Order. Educated at the universities of Naples, Paris, and Cologne, and studying under St. Albert the Great, Aquinas brought a masterful contemplative sense for philosophical and theological realities to everything he studied. The following selection comes from his *Summa Theologiae*, left unfinished at his death. It shows that Christian prayer is about learning to live not simply in this world, but rather learning to live so as to embrace eternal life in the Trinity. Such eternal life can, Aquinas teaches, be tasted even in this life.

Article 1: Whether the soul of man is carried away to things divine?

Objection 1. It would seem that the soul of man is not carried away to things divine. For some define rapture as "an uplifting by the power of a higher nature, from that which is according to nature to that which is above nature." Now it is in accordance with man's nature that he be uplifted to things divine; for Augustine says at the beginning of his *Confessions*: "Thou madest us, Lord, for Thyself, and our heart is restless, till it rest in Thee." Therefore man's soul is not carried away to things divine.

From *Summa Theologiae* II–II, q. 175, aa. 1–6: Of Rapture.

Objection 2. Further, Dionysius says (*Div. Nom.* viii) that "God's justice is seen in this that He treats all things according to their mode and dignity." But it is not in accordance with man's mode and worth that he be raised above what he is according to nature. Therefore it would seem that man's soul is not carried away to things divine.

Objection 3. Further, rapture denotes violence of some kind. But God rules us not by violence or force, as Damascene says (*De Fide Orth.* ii, 30). Therefore man's soul is not carried away to things divine.

On the contrary, The Apostle says (2 Cor. 12:2): "I know a man in Christ . . . rapt even to the third heaven." On which words a gloss says: "Rapt, that is to say, uplifted contrary to nature."

I answer that, Rapture denotes violence of a kind as stated above (obj. 3); and "the violent is that which has its principle without, and in which he that suffers violence concurs not at all" (*Ethic.* iii, 1). Now everything concurs in that to which it tends in accordance with its proper inclination, whether voluntary or natural. Wherefore he who is carried away by some external agent, must be carried to something different from that to which his inclination tends. This difference arises in two ways: in one way from the end of the inclination—for instance a stone, which is naturally inclined to be borne downwards, may be thrown upwards; in another way from the manner of tending—for instance a stone may be thrown downwards with greater velocity than consistent with its natural movement.

Accordingly man's soul also is said to be carried away, in a twofold manner, to that which is contrary to its nature: in one way, as regards the term of transport—as when it is carried away to punishment, according to Ps. 49:22, "Lest He snatch you away, and there be none to deliver you"; in another way, as regards the manner connatural to man, which is that he should understand the truth through sensible things. Hence when he is withdrawn from the apprehension of sensibles, he is said to be carried away, even though he be uplifted to things whereunto he is directed naturally: provided this be not done intentionally, as when a man betakes himself to sleep which is in accordance with nature, wherefore sleep cannot be called rapture, properly speaking.

This withdrawal, whatever its term may be, may arise from a threefold cause. First, from a bodily cause, as happens to those who suffer abstraction from the senses through weakness: secondly, by the power of the demons, as in those who are possessed: thirdly, by the power of God. In this last sense we are now speaking of rapture, whereby a man is uplifted by the spirit of God to things supernatural, and withdrawn from his senses, according to Ezek. 8:3, "The spirit lifted me up between the earth and the heaven, and brought me in the vision of God into Jerusalem."

It must be observed, however, that sometimes a person is said to be carried away, not only through being withdrawn from his senses, but also through being withdrawn from the things to which he was attending, as when a person's mind wanders contrary to his purpose. But this is to use the expression in a less proper signification.

Reply to Objection 1. It is natural to man to tend to divine things through the apprehension of things sensible, according to Rm. 1:20, "The invisible things of God . . . are clearly seen, being understood by the things that are made." But the mode, whereby a man is uplifted to divine things and withdrawn from his senses, is not natural to man.

Reply to Objection 2. It belongs to man's mode and dignity that he be uplifted to divine things, from the very fact that he is made to God's image. And since a divine good infinitely surpasses the faculty of man in order to attain that good, he needs the divine assistance which is bestowed on him in every gift of grace. Hence it is not contrary to nature, but above the faculty of nature that man's mind be thus uplifted in rapture by God.

Reply to Objection 3. The saying of Damascene refers to those things which a man does by himself. But as to those things which are beyond the scope of the free-will, man needs to be uplifted by a stronger operation, which in a certain respect may be called force if we consider the mode of operation, but not if we consider its term to which man is directed both by nature and by his intention.

Article 2: Whether rapture pertains to the cognitive rather than to the appetitive power?

Objection 1. It would seem that rapture pertains to the appetitive rather than to the cognitive power. For Dionysius says (*Div. Nom.* iv): "The Divine love causes ecstasy." Now love pertains to the appetitive power. Therefore so does ecstasy or rapture.

Objection 2. Further, Gregory says (*Dial.* ii, 3) that "he who fed the swine debased himself by a dissipated mind and an unclean life; whereas Peter, when the angel delivered him and carried him into ecstasy, was not beside himself, but above himself." Now the prodigal son sank into the depths by his appetite. Therefore in those also who are carried up into the heights it is the appetite that is affected.

Objection 3. Further, a gloss on Ps. 30:1, "In Thee, O Lord, have I hoped, let me never be confounded," says in explaining the title [Unto the end, a psalm for David, in an ecstasy]: "Ekstasis in Greek signifies in Latin 'excessus mentis,' an aberration of the mind. This happens in two ways, either through dread of earthly things or through the mind being rapt in heavenly things and forgetful of this lower world." Now dread of earthly things pertains to the appetite. Therefore rapture of the mind in heavenly things, being placed in opposition to this dread, also pertains to the appetite.

On the contrary, A gloss on Ps. 115:2, "I said in my excess: Every man is a liar," says: "We speak of ecstasy, not when the mind wanders through fear, but when it is carried aloft on the wings of revelation." Now revelation pertains to the intellective power. Therefore ecstasy or rapture does also.

I answer that, We can speak of rapture in two ways. First, with regard to the term of rapture, and thus, properly speaking, rapture cannot pertain to the appetitive, but only to the cognitive power. For it was stated (a. 1) that rapture is outside the inclination of the person who is rapt; whereas the movement of the appetitive power is an inclination to an appetible good. Wherefore, properly speaking, in desiring something, a man is not rapt, but is moved by himself.

Secondly, rapture may be considered with regard to its cause, and thus it may have a cause on the part of the appetitive power. For from the very fact that the appetite is strongly affected towards something, it may happen, owing to the violence of his affection, that a man is carried away from everything else. Moreover, it has an effect on the appetitive power, when for instance a man delights in the things to which he is rapt. Hence the Apostle said that he was rapt, not only "to the third heaven"—which pertains to the contemplation of the intellect—but also into "paradise," which pertains to the appetite.

Reply to Objection 1. Rapture adds something to ecstasy. For ecstasy means simply a going out of oneself by being placed outside one's proper order; while rapture denotes a certain violence in addition. Accordingly ecstasy may pertain to the appetitive power, as when a man's appetite tends to something outside him, and in this sense Dionysius says that "the Divine love causes ecstasy," inasmuch as it makes man's appetite tend to the object loved. Hence he says afterwards that "even God Himself, the cause of all things, through the overflow of His loving goodness, goes outside Himself in His providence for all beings." But even if this were said expressly of rapture, it would merely signify that love is the cause of rapture.

Reply to Objection 2. There is a twofold appetite in man; to wit, the intellective appetite which is called the will, and the sensitive appetite known as the sensuality. Now it is proper to man that his lower appetite be subject to the higher appetite, and that the higher move the lower. Hence man may become outside himself as regards the appetite, in two ways. In one way, when a man's intellective appetite tends wholly to divine things, and takes no account of those things whereto the sensitive appetite inclines him; thus Dionysius says (*Div. Nom.* iv) that "Paul being in ecstasy through the vehemence of Divine love" exclaimed: "I live, now not I, but Christ liveth in me."

In another way, when a man tends wholly to things pertaining to the lower appetite, and takes no account of his higher appetite. It is thus that "he who fed the swine debased himself"; and this latter kind of going out of oneself, or being beside oneself, is more akin than the former to the nature of rapture because the higher appetite is more proper to man. Hence when through the violence of his lower appetite a man is withdrawn from the movement of his higher appetite, it is more a case of being withdrawn from that which is proper to him. Yet, because there is no violence therein, since the will is able to resist the passion, it falls short of the true nature of rapture, unless perchance the passion be so strong that it takes away entirely the use of reason, as happens to those who are mad with anger or love.

It must be observed, however, that both these excesses affecting the appetite may cause an excess in the cognitive power, either because the mind is carried away to certain intelligible objects, through being drawn away from objects of sense, or because it is caught up into some imaginary vision or fanciful apparition.

Reply to Objection 3. Just as love is a movement of the appetite with regard to good, so fear is a movement of the appetite with regard to evil. Wherefore either of them may equally cause an aberration of mind; and all the more since fear arises from love, as Augustine says (*De Civ. Dei* xiv, 7,9).

Article 3: Whether Paul, when in rapture, saw the essence of God?

Objection 1. It would seem that Paul, when in rapture, did not see the essence of God. For just as we read of Paul that he was rapt to the third heaven, so we read of Peter (Acts 10:10) that "there came upon him an ecstasy of mind." Now Peter, in his ecstasy, saw not God's essence but an imaginary vision. Therefore it would seem that neither did Paul see the essence of God.

Objection 2. Further, the vision of God is beatific. But Paul, in his rapture, was not beatified; else he would never have returned to the unhappiness of this life, but his body would have been glorified by the overflow from his soul, as will happen to the saints after the resurrection, and this clearly was not the case. Therefore Paul when in rapture saw not the essence of God.

Objection 3. Further, according to 1 Cor. 13:10–12, faith and hope are incompatible with the vision of the Divine essence. But Paul when in this state had faith and hope. Therefore he saw not the essence of God.

Objection 4. Further, as Augustine states (*Gen. ad lit.* xii, 6,7), "pictures of bodies are seen in the imaginary vision." Now Paul is stated (2 Cor. 12:2,4) to have seen certain pictures in his rapture, for instance of the "third heaven" and of "paradise." Therefore he would seem to have been rapt to an imaginary vision rather than to the vision of the Divine essence.

On the contrary, Augustine (*Ep.* CXLVII, 13; *ad Paulin., de videndo Deum*) concludes that "possibly God's very substance was seen by some while yet in this life: for instance by Moses, and by Paul who in rapture heard unspeakable words, which it is not granted unto man to utter."

I answer that, Some have said that Paul, when in rapture, saw "not the very essence of God, but a certain reflection of His clarity." But Augustine clearly comes to an opposite decision, not only in his book (*De videndo Deum*), but also in *Gen. ad lit.* xii, 28 (quoted in a gloss on 2 Cor. 12:2). Indeed the words themselves of the Apostle indicate this. For he says that "he heard secret words, which it is not granted unto man to utter": and such would seem to be words pertaining to the vision of the blessed, which transcends the state of the wayfarer, according to Is. 64:4, "Eye hath not seen, O God, besides Thee, what things Thou hast prepared for them that love [Vulg.: 'wait for'] Thee" [cf. 1 Cor. 2:9]. Therefore it is more becoming to hold that he saw God in His essence.

Reply to Objection 1. Man's mind is rapt by God to the contemplation of divine truth in three ways. First, so that he contemplates it through certain imaginary pictures, and such was the ecstasy that came upon Peter. Secondly, so that he contemplates the divine truth through its intelligible effects; such was the ecstasy of David, who said (Ps. 115:11): "I said in my excess: Every man is a liar." Thirdly, so that he contemplates it in its essence. Such was the rapture of Paul, as also of Moses [cf. II–II, q. 174, a. 4]; and not without reason, since as Moses was the first Teacher of the Jews, so was Paul the first "Teacher of the gentiles."

Reply to Objection 2. The Divine essence cannot be seen by a created intellect save through the light of glory, of which it is written (Ps. 35:10): "In Thy light we shall see light." But this light can be shared in two ways. First by way of an abiding form, and thus it beatifies the saints in heaven. Secondly, by way of a transitory passion, as stated above (II–II, q. 171, a. 2) of the light of prophecy; and in this way that light was in Paul when he was in rapture. Hence this vision did not beatify him simply, so as to overflow into his body, but only in a restricted sense. Consequently this rapture pertains somewhat to prophecy.

Reply to Objection 3. Since, in his rapture, Paul was beatified not as to the habit, but only as to the act of the blessed, it follows that he had not the act of faith at the same time, although he had the habit.

Reply to Objection 4. In one way by the third heaven we may understand something corporeal, and thus the third heaven denotes the empyrean, which is described as the "third," in relation to the aerial and starry heavens, or better still, in relation to the aqueous and crystalline heavens. Moreover Paul is stated to be rapt to the "third heaven," not as though his rapture consisted in the vision of something corporeal, but because this place is appointed for the contemplation of the blessed. Hence the gloss on 2 Cor. 12 says that the "third heaven is a spiritual heaven, where the angels and the holy souls enjoy the contemplation of God: and when Paul says that he was rapt to this heaven he means that God showed him the life wherein He is to be seen forevermore."

In another way the third heaven may signify a supramundane vision. Such a vision may be called the third heaven in three ways. First, according to the order of the cognitive powers. In this way the first heaven would indicate a supramundane bodily vision, conveyed through the senses; thus was seen the hand of one writing on the wall (Dan. 5:5); the second heaven would be an imaginary vision such as Isaiah saw, and John in the Apocalypse; and the third heaven would denote an intellectual vision according to Augustine's explanation (*Gen. ad lit.* xii, 26,28,34). Secondly, the third heaven may be taken according to the order of things knowable, the first heaven being "the knowledge of heavenly bodies, the second the knowledge of heavenly spirits, the third the knowledge of God Himself." Thirdly, the third heaven may denote the contemplation of God according to the degrees of knowledge whereby God is seen. The first of these degrees belongs to the angels of the lowest hierarchy, the second to the angels of the middle hierarchy, the third to the angels of the highest hierarchy, according to the gloss on 2 Cor. 12.

And since the vision of God cannot be without delight, he says that he was not only "rapt to the third heaven" by reason of his contemplation, but also into "Paradise" by reason of the consequent delight.

Article 4: Whether Paul, when in rapture, was withdrawn from his senses?

Objection 1. It would seem that Paul, when in rapture, was not withdrawn from his senses. For Augustine says (*Gen. ad lit.* xii, 28): "Why should we not believe that when so great an apostle, the teacher of the gentiles, was rapt to this most sublime vision, God was willing to vouchsafe him a glimpse of that eternal life which is to take the place of the present life?" Now in that future life after the resurrection the saints will see the Divine essence without being withdrawn from the senses of the body. Therefore neither did such a withdrawal take place in Paul.

Objection 2. Further, Christ was truly a wayfarer, and also enjoyed an uninterrupted vision of the Divine essence, without, however, being withdrawn from His senses. Therefore there was no need for Paul to be withdrawn from his senses in order for him to see the essence of God.

Objection 3. Further, after seeing God in His essence, Paul remembered what he had seen in that vision; hence he said (2 Cor. 12:4): "He heard secret words, which it is not granted to man to utter." Now the memory belongs to the sensitive faculty according to the Philosopher (*De Mem. et Remin.* i). Therefore it seems that Paul, while seeing the essence of God, was not withdrawn from his senses.

On the contrary, Augustine says (*Gen. ad lit.* xii, 27): "Unless a man in some way depart this life, whether by going altogether out of his body or by turning away and withdrawing from his carnal senses, so that he truly knows not as the Apostle said, whether he be in the body or out of the body, he is not rapt and caught up into that vision."

I answer that, The Divine essence cannot be seen by man through any cognitive power other than the intellect. Now the human intellect does not turn to intelligible objects except by means of the phantasms which it takes from the senses through the intelligible species; and it is in considering these phantasms that the intellect judges of and coordinates sensible objects. Hence in any operation that requires abstraction of the intellect from phantasms, there must be also withdrawal of the intellect from the senses. Now in the state of the wayfarer it is necessary for man's intellect, if it see God's essence, to be withdrawn from phantasms. For God's essence cannot be seen by means of a phantasm, nor indeed by any created intelligible species, since God's essence infinitely transcends not only all bodies, which are represented by phantasms, but also all intelligible creatures. Now when man's intellect is uplifted to the sublime vision of God's essence, it is necessary that his mind's whole attention should be summoned to that purpose in such a way that he understand naught else by phantasms, and be absorbed entirely in God. Therefore it is impossible for man while a wayfarer to see God in His essence without being withdrawn from his senses.

Reply to Objection 1. As stated above (a. 3, obj. 2), after the resurrection, in the blessed who see God in His essence, there will be an overflow from the intellect to the lower powers and even to the body. Hence it is in keeping with the rule itself of the divine vision that the soul will turn towards phantasms and sensible objects. But there is no such overflow in those who are raptured, as stated (a. 3, obj. 2, ad 2), and consequently the comparison fails.

Reply to Objection 2. The intellect of Christ's soul was glorified by the habit of the light of glory, whereby He saw the Divine essence much more fully than an angel or a man. He was, however, a wayfarer on account of the passibility of His body, in respect of which He was "made a little lower than the angels" (Heb. 2:9), by dispensation, and not on account of any defect on the part of His intellect. Hence there is no comparison between Him and other wayfarers.

Reply to Objection 3. Paul, after seeing God in His essence, remembered what he had known in that vision, by means of certain intelligible species that remained in his intellect by way of habit; even as in the absence of the sensible object, certain impressions remain in the soul which it recollects when it turns to the phantasms. And so this was the knowledge that he was unable wholly to think over or express in words.

Article 5: Whether, while in this state, Paul's soul was wholly separated from his body?

Objection 1. It would seem that, while in this state, Paul's soul was wholly separated from his body. For the Apostle says (2 Cor. 5:6,7): "While we are in the body we are absent from the Lord. For we walk by faith, and not by sight." Now, while in that state, Paul was not absent from the Lord, for he saw Him by a species, as stated above (a. 3). Therefore he was not in the body.

Objection 2. Further, a power of the soul cannot be uplifted above the soul's essence wherein it is rooted. Now in this rapture the intellect, which is a power of the soul, was withdrawn from its bodily surroundings through being uplifted to divine contemplation. Much more therefore was the essence of the soul separated from the body.

Objection 3. Further, the forces of the vegetative soul are more material than those of the sensitive soul. Now in order for him to be rapt to the vision of God, it was necessary for him to be withdrawn from the forces of the sensitive soul, as stated above (a. 4). Much more, therefore, was it necessary for him to be withdrawn from the forces of the vegetative soul. Now when these forces cease to operate, the soul is no longer in any way united to the body. Therefore it would seem that in Paul's rapture it was necessary for the soul to be wholly separated from the body.

On the contrary, Augustine says (*Ep.* CXLVII, 13, *ad Paulin, de videndo Deum*): "It is not incredible that this sublime revelation" (namely, that they should see God in His essence) "was vouchsafed certain saints, without their departing this life so completely as to leave nothing but a corpse for burial." Therefore it was not necessary for Paul's soul, when in rapture, to be wholly separated from his body.

I answer that, As stated above (a. 1, obj. 1), in the rapture of which we are speaking now, man is uplifted by God's power, "from that which is according to nature to that which is above nature." Wherefore two things have to be considered: first, what pertains to man according to nature; secondly, what has to be done by God in man above his nature. Now, since the soul is united to the body as its natural form, it belongs to the soul to have a natural disposition to understand by turning to phantasms; and this is not withdrawn by the divine power from the soul in rapture, since its state undergoes no change, as stated above (a. 3, ad 2,3). Yet, this state remaining, actual conversion to phantasms and sensible objects is withdrawn from the soul, lest it be hindered from being uplifted to that which transcends all phantasms, as stated above (a. 4). Therefore it was not necessary that his soul in rapture should be so separated from the body as to cease to be united thereto as its form; and yet it was necessary for his intellect to be withdrawn from phantasms and the perception of sensible objects.

Reply to Objection 1. In this rapture Paul was absent from the Lord as regards his state, since he was still in the state of a wayfarer, but not as regards the act by which he saw God by a species, as stated above (a. 3, ad 2,3).

Reply to Objection 2. A faculty of the soul is not uplifted by the natural power above the mode becoming the essence of the soul; but it can be uplifted by the divine power to something higher, even as a body by the violence of a stronger power is lifted up above the place befitting it according to its specific nature.

Reply to Objection 3. The forces of the vegetative soul do not operate through the soul being intent thereon, as do the sensitive forces, but by way of nature. Hence in the case of rapture there is no need for withdrawal from them, as from the sensitive powers, whose operations would lessen the intentness of the soul on intellective knowledge.

Article 6: Did Paul know whether his soul was separated from his body?

Objection 1. It would seem that Paul was not ignorant whether his soul was separated from his body. For he says (2 Cor. 12:2): "I know a man in Christ rapt even to the third heaven." Now man denotes something composed of soul and body; and rapture differs from death. Seemingly therefore he knew that his soul was not separated from his body by death, which is the more probable seeing that this is the common opinion of the Doctors.

Objection 2. Further, it appears from the same words of the Apostle that he knew whither he was rapt, since it was "to the third heaven." Now this shows that he knew whether he was in the body or not, for if he knew the third heaven to be something corporeal, he must have known that his soul was not separated from his body, since a corporeal thing cannot be an object of sight save through the body. Therefore it would seem that he was not ignorant whether his soul was separated from his body.

Objection 3. Further, Augustine says (*Gen. ad lit.* xii, 28) that "when in rapture, he saw God with the same vision as the saints see Him in heaven." Now from the very fact that the saints see God, they know whether their soul is separated from their body. Therefore Paul too knew this.

On the contrary, It is written (2 Cor. 12:3): "Whether in the body, or out of the body, I know not, God knoweth."

I answer that, The true answer to this question must be gathered from the Apostle's very words, whereby he says he knew something, namely that he was "rapt even to the third heaven," and that something he knew not, namely "whether" he were "in the body or out of the body." This may be understood in two ways. First, the words "whether in the body or out of the body" may refer not to the very being of the man who was rapt (as though he knew not whether his soul were in his body or not), but to the mode of rapture, so that he ignored whether his body besides his soul, or, on the other hand, his soul alone, were rapt to the third heaven. Thus Ezekiel is stated (Ezek. 8:3) to have been "brought in the vision of God into Jerusalem." This was the explanation of a certain Jew according to Jerome (*Prolog. super Daniel.*), where he says that "lastly our Apostle" (thus said the Jew) "durst not assert that he was rapt in his body, but said: 'Whether in the body or out of the body, I know not.'"

Augustine, however, disapproves of this explanation (*Gen. ad lit.* xii, 3) for the reason that the Apostle states that he knew he was rapt even to the third heaven. Wherefore he knew it to be really the third heaven to which he was rapt, and not an imaginary likeness of the third heaven: otherwise if he gave the name of third heaven to an imaginary third heaven, in the same way he might state that he was rapt in the body, meaning, by body, an image of his body, such as appears in one's dreams. Now if he knew it to be really the third heaven, it follows that either he knew it to be something spiritual and incorporeal, and then his body could not be rapt thither; or he knew it to be something corporeal, and then his soul could not be rapt thither without his body, unless it were separated from his body. Consequently we must explain the matter otherwise, by saying that the Apostle knew himself to be rapt both in soul and body, but that he ignored how his soul stood in relation to his body, to wit, whether it was accompanied by his body or not.

Here we find a diversity of opinions. For some say that the Apostle knew his soul to be united to his body as its form, but ignored whether it was abstracted from its senses, or again whether it was abstracted from the operations of the vegetative soul. But he could not but know that it was abstracted from the senses, seeing that he knew himself to be rapt; and as to his being abstracted from the operation of the vegetative soul, this was not of such importance as to require him to be so careful in mentioning it. It follows, then, that the Apostle ignored whether his soul was united to his body as its form, or separated from it by death. Some, however, granting this, say that the Apostle did not consider the matter while he was in rapture, because he was wholly intent upon God, but that afterwards he questioned the point, when taking cognizance of what he had seen. But this also is contrary to the Apostle's words, for he there distinguishes between the past and what happened subsequently, since he states that at the present time he knows that he was rapt "four-teen years ago," and that at the present time he knows not "whether he was in the body or out of the body."

Consequently we must assert that both before and after he ignored whether his soul was separated from his body. Wherefore Augustine (*Gen. ad lit.* xii, 5), after discussing the question at length, concludes: "Perhaps then we must infer that he ignored whether, when he was rapt to the third heaven, his soul was in his body (in the same way as the soul is in the body, when we speak of a living body either of a waking or of a sleeping man, or of one that is withdrawn from his bodily senses during ecstasy), or whether his soul went out of his body altogether, so that his body lay dead."

Reply to Objection 1. Sometimes by the figure of synecdoche a part of man, especially the soul which is the principal part, denotes a man. Or again we might take this to mean that he whom he states to have been rapt was a man not at the time of his rapture, but fourteen years after-wards: for he says "I know a man," not "I know a rapt man." Again noth-ing hinders death brought about by God being called rapture; and thus Augustine says (*Gen. ad lit.* xii, 3): "If the Apostle doubted the matter, who of us will dare to be certain about it?" Wherefore those who have something to say on this subject speak with more conjecture than cer-tainty.

Reply to Objection 2. The Apostle knew that either the heaven in ques-tion was something incorporeal, or that he saw something incorporeal in that heaven; yet this could be done by his intellect, even without his soul being separated from his body.

Reply to Objection 3. Paul's vision, while he was in rapture, was like the vision of the blessed in one respect, namely as to the thing seen; and, un-like, in another respect, namely as to the mode of seeing, because he saw not so perfectly as do the saints in heaven. Hence Augustine says (*Gen. ad lit.* xii, 36): "Although, when the Apostle was rapt from his carnal senses to the third heaven, he lacked that full and perfect knowledge of things which is in the angels, in that he knew not whether he was in the body, or out of the body, this will surely not be lacking after reunion with the body in the resurrection of the dead, when this corruptible will put on incorruption."

Questions

1. What is "rapture," as described by St. Thomas?
2. Can a person, while living on earth, see by contemplation the divine essence, God as he is in himself? How is this possible?
3. How does rapture involve the intellect and will?

St. Gregory of Sinai

St. Gregory of Sinai, who died in what is now Bulgaria in 1346, traveled extensively in order to learn the monastic life. Among other places, he lived in Cyprus, Mt. Sinai, Palestine, Crete, and Mt. Athos. In 1325 he founded a monastery on Mt. Paroria, in Bulgaria, and his influence spread throughout the Christian East. A great spiritual writer influenced by St. John Climacus, St. Gregory of Sinai describes in the following excerpt the ascetical practices necessary for fruitful prayer and proposes modes of vocal prayer—primarily the repetition of the name of Jesus and chanting psalms—that lead to contemplative fullness.

Two Ways of Prayer

THERE ARE TWO MODES OF UNION OR, rather, two ways of entering into the noetic prayer that the Spirit activates in the heart. For either the intellect, cleaving to the Lord (cf. 1 Cor. 6:17), is present in the heart prior to the action of the prayer; or the prayer itself, progressively quickened in the fire of spiritual joy, draws the intellect along with it or welds

From "On Stillness: Fifteen Texts," in *The Philokalia*, compiled by St. Nikodimos of the Holy Mountain and St. Makarios of Corinth, vol. 4, trans. and ed. by G. E. H. Palmer, Philip Sherrard, and Kallistos Ware (London: Faber and Faber, 1995), 262–74.

it to the invocation of the Lord Jesus and to union with Him. For since the Spirit works in each person as He wishes (cf. 1 Cor. 12:11), one of these two ways we have mentioned will take precedence in some people, the other in others. Sometimes, as the passions subside through the ceaseless invocation of Jesus Christ, a divine energy wells up in the heart, and a divine warmth is kindled; for Scripture says that our God is a fire that consumes the passions (cf. Deut. 4:24; Heb. 12:29). At other times the Spirit draws the intellect to Himself, confining it to the depth of the heart and restraining it from its usual distractions. Then it will no longer be led captive from Jerusalem to the Assyrians, but a change for the better brings it back from Babylon to Zion, so that it says with the Psalmist, "It is right to praise Thee, O God, in Zion, and to Thee shall our vows be rendered in Jerusalem" (Ps. 65:1. LXX), and "When the Lord brought back the prisoners to Zion" (Ps. 126:1), and "Jacob will rejoice and Israel will be glad" (Ps. 53:6). The names Jacob and Israel refer respectively to the ascetically active and to the contemplative intellect which through ascetic labour and with God's help overcomes the passions and through contemplation sees God, so far as is possible. Then the intellect, as if invited to a rich banquet and replete with divine joy, will sing, "Thou has prepared a table before me in the face of the demons and passions that afflict me" (cf. Ps. 23:5).

The Beginning of Watchfulness

"In the morning sow your seed," says Solomon—and by "seed" is to be understood the seed of prayer—"and in the evening do not withhold your hand," so that there may be no break in the continuity of your prayer, no moment when through lack of attention you cease to pray, "for you do not know which will flourish, this or that" (Eccles. 11:6). Sitting from dawn on a seat about nine inches high, compel your intellect to descend from your head into your heart, and retain it there. Keeping your head forcibly bent downwards, and suffering acute pain in your chest, shoulders and neck, persevere in repeating noetically or in your soul "Lord Jesus Christ, have mercy." Then, since that may become constrictive and wearisome, and even galling because of the constant repetition—though this is not because you are constantly eating the one food of the threefold name, for "those who eat Me," says Scripture, "will still be hungry" (Eccles. 24:21)—let your intellect concentrate on the second half of the prayer and repeat the words "Son of God, have mercy." You must say this half over and over again and not out of laziness constantly change the words. For plants which are frequently transplanted do not put down roots. Restrain your breathing, so as not to breathe unimpededly; for when you exhale, the air, rising from the heart, beclouds the intellect and ruffles your thinking, keeping the intellect away from the heart. Then the intellect is either enslaved by forgetfulness or induced to give its attention to all manner of things, insensibly becoming preoccupied with what it should ignore. If you see impure evil thoughts rising up and assuming various forms in your intellect, do not be startled. Even if images of good things appear to you, pay no attention to them. But restraining your breathing as much as possible and enclosing your intellect in your heart, invoke the Lord Jesus continuously and diligently and you will swiftly consume and subdue them, flaying them invisibly with the divine name. For St. John Klimakos says, "With the name of Jesus lash your enemies, for there is no more powerful weapon in heaven or on earth."

Isaiah the Solitary is one of many who affirm that when praying you have to restrain your breath. Another author says that you have to control your uncontrollable intellect, impelled and dispersed as it is by the satanic power which seizes hold of your lax soul because of your negligence after baptism, bringing with it other spirits even more evil than itself and thus making your soul's state worse than it was originally (cf. Matt. 12:45). Another writer says that in a monk mindfulness of God ought to take the place of breathing, while another declares that the love of God acts as a brake on his out-breathing. St. Symeon the New Theologian tells us, "Restrain the drawing-in of breath through your nostrils, so as not to breathe easily"; St. John Klimakos says, "Let mindfulness of Jesus be united to your breathing, and then you will know the blessings of stillness." St. Paul affirms that it is not he who lives but Christ in him (cf. Gal. 2:20), activating him and inspiring him with divine life. And the Lord, taking as an example the blowing of the physical wind, says, "The Spirit blows where He wishes" (John 3:8). For when we were cleansed through baptism we received in seed-like form the foretaste of the Spirit (cf. 2 Cor. 1:22) and what St. James calls the "implanted Logos" (James 1:21), embedded and as it were consolidated in us through an unparticipable participation; and, while keeping Himself inviolate and undiminished, He deifies us in His superabundant bounty. But then we neglected the commandments, the guardians of grace, and through this neglect we again fell into the clutches of the passions, filled with the afflatus of the evil spirits instead of the breath of the Holy Spirit. That is why, as the holy fathers explain, we are subject to lassitude and continually enervated. For had we laid hold of the Spirit and been purified by Him we would have been enkindled by Him and inspired with divine life, and would speak and think and act in the manner that the Lord indicates when He says, "For it is not you that speak but the Spirit of My Father that speaks in you" (cf. Matt. 10:20). Conversely, if we embrace the devil and are mastered by him, we speak and act in the opposite manner.

"When the watchman grows weary," says St. John Klimakos, "he stands up and prays; then he sits down again and courageously resumes the same task." Although St. John is here referring to the intellect and is saying that it should behave in this manner when it has learnt how to guard the heart, yet what he says can apply equally to psalmody. For it is said that when the great Varsanuphios was asked about how one should psalmodize, he replied, "The Hours and the liturgical Odes are church traditions, rightly given so that concord is maintained when there are many praying together. But the monks of Sketis do not recite the Hours, nor do they sing Odes. On their own they practice manual labour, meditation and a little prayer. When you stand in prayer, you should repeat the Trisagion and the Lord's Prayer. You should also ask God to deliver you from your fallen selfhood. Do not grow slack in doing this; your mind should be concentrated in prayer all day long." What St. Varsanuphios wanted to make clear is that private meditation is the prayer of the heart, and that to practice "a little prayer" means to stand and psalmodize. Moreover, St. John Klimakos explicitly says that to attain the state of stillness entails first total detachment, secondly resolute prayer—this means standing and psalmodizing—and thirdly, unbroken labour of the heart, that is to say, sitting down to pray in stillness.

Different Ways of Psalmodizing

Why do some teach that we should psalmodize a lot, others a little, and others that we should not psalmodize at all but should devote ourselves only to prayer and to physical exertion such as manual labour, prostrations or some other strenuous activity? The explanation is as follows. Those who have found grace through long, arduous practice of the ascetic life teach others to find it in the same way. They do not believe that there are some who through cognitive insight and fervent faith have by the mercy of God attained the state of grace in a short time, as St. Isaac, for instance, recognizes. Led astray by ignorance and self-conceit they disparage such people, claiming that anything different from their own experience is delusion and not the operation of grace. They do not know that "it is easy for God to enrich a poor man suddenly" (Eccles. 11:21), and that "wisdom is the principal thing; therefore acquire wisdom," as Proverbs says, referring to grace (4:7). Similarly St. Paul is rebuking the disciples of his time who were ignorant of grace when he says, "Do you not realize that Jesus Christ dwells within you, unless you are worthless?" (cf. 2 Cor. 13:5)—unless, that is to say, you make no progress because of your negligence. Thus in their disbelief and arrogance they do not acknowledge the exceptional qualities of prayer activated in some people by the Spirit in a special way.

Objection: Tell me, if a person fasts, practices self-control, keeps vigils, stands, makes prostrations, grieves inwardly and lives in poverty, is this not active asceticism? How then do you advocate simply the singing of psalms, yet say that without ascetic labour it is impossible to succeed in prayer? Do not the activities I mention constitute ascetic labour?

Answer: If you pray with your lips but your mind wanders, how do you benefit? "When one builds and another tears down, what do they gain but toil?" (Eccles. 34:23). As you labour with your body, so you must labour with your intellect, lest you appear righteous in the body while your heart is filled with every form of injustice and impurity. St. Paul confirms this when he says that if he prays with his tongue—that is, with his lips—his spirit or his voice prays, but his intellect is unproductive: "I will pray with my spirit, and I will also pray with my intellect" (cf. 1 Cor. 14:14–15). And he adds, "I would rather speak five words with my intellect than ten thousand with my tongue" (cf. 1 Cor. 14:19). St. John Klimakos, too, indicates that St. Paul is speaking here about prayer when he says in his chapter on prayer, "The great practitioner of sublime and perfect prayer says, 'I would rather speak five words with my intellect.'" There are many other forms of spiritual work, yet not one in itself is all-sufficient; but prayer of the heart, according to St. John Klimakos, is pre-eminent and all-embracing, the source of the virtues and catalyst of all goodness. "There is nothing more fearful than the thought of death," says St. Maximos, "or more wonderful than mindfulness of God," indicating the supremacy of this activity. But some do not even wish to know that we can attain a state of active grace in this present life, so blinded and weak in faith are they because of their ignorance and obduracy.

In my opinion, those who do not psalmodize much act rightly, for it means that they esteem moderation—and according to the sages moderation is best in all things. In this way they do not expend all the energy of their soul in ascetic labour, thus making the intellect negligent and slack where prayer is concerned. On the contrary, by devoting but little time to psalmodizing, they can give most of their time to prayer. On the other hand, when the intellect is exhausted by continuous noetic invocation and intense concentration, it can be given some rest by releasing it from the straitness of silent prayer and allowing it to relax in the amplitude of psalmody. This is an excellent rule, taught by the wisest men.

Those who do not psalmodize at all also act rightly, provided they are well advanced on the spiritual path. Such people have no need to recite psalms; if they have attained the state of illumination, they should cultivate silence, uninterrupted prayer and contemplation. They are united with God and have no need to tear their intellect away from Him and so to throw it into confusion. As St. John Klimakos says, "One under monastic obedience falls when he follows his own will, while the hesychast falls when he is interrupted in his prayer." For the hesychast commits adultery in his intellect when he sunders it from its mindfulness of God: it is as if he were being unfaithful to his true spouse and philandering with trivial matters.

To impart this discipline to others is not always possible. But it can be taught to simple uneducated people who are under obedience to a spiritual father, for such obedience, thanks to the humility that goes with it, can partake of every virtue. Those, however, who are not under this kind of obedience should not be taught it, regardless of whether they are unlearned people or educated: they may easily be deluded, because people who are a law unto themselves cannot avoid being conceited, and the natural result of conceit is delusion, as St. Isaac says. Yet some people, unaware of the harm which will result, counsel anybody they happen to meet to practice this discipline alone, so that their intellect may grow accustomed to being mindful of God and may come to love it. But this is not possible, especially for those not under obedience. For, because of their negligence and arrogance, their intellect is still impure and has not first been cleansed by tears; and so, instead of concentrating on prayer, they are filled with images of shameful thoughts, while the unclean spirits in their heart, panic-struck by the invocation of the dread name of the Lord Jesus, howl for the destruction of the person who scourges them. Thus if you hear about or are taught this discipline, and want to practise it, but are not under spiritual direction you will experience one of two things: you will either force yourself to persist, in which case you fall into delusion and will fail to attain healing; or you will grow negligent, in which case you will never make any progress during your whole life.

I will add this from my own small experience. When you sit in stillness, by day or by night, free from random thoughts and continuously praying to God in humility, you may find that your intellect becomes exhausted through calling upon God and that your body and heart begin to feel pain because of the intense concentration with which you unceasingly invoke the name of Jesus, with the result that you no longer experience the warmth and joy that engender ardour and patience in the spiritual aspirant. If this is the case, stand up and psalmodize, either by yourself or with a disciple who lives with you, or occupy yourself with meditation on some scriptural passage or with the remembrance of death, or with manual labour or with some other thing, or give your attention to reading, preferably standing up so as to involve your body in the task as well.

When you stand and psalmodize by yourself, recite the Trisagion and then pray in your soul or your intellect, making your intellect pay attention to your heart; and recite two or three psalms and a few penitential *troparia* but without chanting them: as St. John Klimakos confirms, people at this stage of spiritual development do not chant. For "the suffering of the heart endured in a spirit of devotion," as St. Mark puts it, is sufficient to produce joy in them, and the warmth of the Spirit is given to them as a source of grace and exultation. After each psalm again pray in your intellect or soul, keeping your thoughts from wandering, and repeat the Alleluia. This is the order established by the holy fathers Varsanuphios, Diadochos and others. And as St. Basil the Great says, one should vary the psalms daily to enkindle one's fervour and to prevent the intellect from getting bored with having to recite always the same things. The intellect should be given freedom and then its fervour will be quickened. If you stand and psalmodize with a trusted disciple, let him recite the psalms while you guard yourself, secretly watching your heart and praying. With the help of prayer ignore all images, whether sensory or conceptual, that rise up from the heart. For stillness means the shedding of all thoughts for a time, even those which are divine and engendered by the Spirit; otherwise through giving them our attention because they are good we will lose what is better.

So, lover of God, attend with care and intelligence. If while engaged in spiritual work you see a light or a fire outside you, or a form supposedly of Christ or of an angel or of someone else, reject it lest you suffer harm. And do not pay court to images, lest you allow them to stamp themselves on your intellect. For all these things that externally and inopportunely assume various guises do so in order to delude your soul. The true beginning of prayer is the warmth of heart that scarifies the passions, fills the soul with joy and delight, and establishes the heart in unwavering love and unhesitating surety. The holy fathers teach that if the heart is in doubt about whether to accept something either sensory or conceptual that enters the soul, then that thing is not from God but has been sent by the devil. Moreover, if you become aware that your intellect is being enticed by some invisible power either from the outside or from above, do not trust in that power or let your intellect be so enticed, but immediately force it to continue its work.

What is of God, says St. Isaac, comes of itself, without you knowing when it will come. Our natural enemy—the demon who operates in the seat of our desiring power—gives the spirit-forces various guises in our imagination. In this way he substitutes his own unruly heat for spiritual warmth, so that the soul is oppressed by this deceit. For spiritual delight he substitutes mindless joy and a muggy sense of pleasure, inducing self-satisfaction and vanity. Thus he tries to conceal himself from those who lack experience and to persuade them to take his delusions for manifestations of spiritual joy. But time, experience and perspicacity will reveal him to those not entirely ignorant of his wiles. As the palate discriminates between different kinds of food (cf. Eccles. 36:18,19), so the spiritual sense of taste clearly and unerringly reveals everything as it truly is.

"Since you are engaged in spiritual warfare," says St. John Klimakos, "you should read texts concerned with ascetic practice. Translating such texts into action makes other reading superfluous." Read works of the fathers related to stillness and prayer, like those of St. John Klimakos, St. Isaac, St. Maximos, St. Neilos, St. Hesychios, Philotheos of Sinai, St. Symeon the New Theologian and his disciple Stithatos, and whatever else exists of writers of this kind. Leave other books for the time being, not because they are to be rejected, but because they do not contribute to your present purpose, diverting the intellect from prayer by their narrative character. Read by yourself, but not in a pompous voice, or with pretentious eloquence or affected enunciation or melodic delectation, or, insensibly carried away by passion, as if you are wanting to please an audience. Do not read with inordinate avidity, for in all things moderation is best, nor on the other hand in a rough, sluggish or negligent manner. On the contrary, read reverently, gently, steadily, with understanding, and at an even pace, your intellect, your soul and your reason all engaged. When the intellect is invigorated by such reading, it acquires the strength to pray harder. But if you read in the contrary manner—as I have described it above—you cloud the intellect and make it sluggish and distracted, so that you develop a headache and grow slack in prayer.

Continually take careful note of your inner intention: watch carefully which way it inclines, and discover whether it is for God and for the sake of goodness itself and the benefit of your soul that you practice stillness or psalmodize or read or pray or cultivate some virtue. Otherwise you may unknowingly be ensnared and prove to be an ascetic in outward appearance alone while in your manner of life and inner intention you are wanting to impress men, and not to conform to God. For the devil's traps are many, and he persistently and secretly watches the bias of our intention, without most of us being aware of it, striving imperceptibly to corrupt our labour so that what we do is not done in accordance with God's will. But even if he attacks and assaults you relentlessly and shamelessly, and even if he distracts the bias of your will and makes it waver in spite of your efforts to prevent it, you will not often be caught out by him so long as you keep yourself steadfastly intent on God. If again in spite of your efforts you are overcome through weakness, you will swiftly be forgiven and praised by Him who knows our intentions and our hearts. There is, however, one passion—self-esteem—that does not permit a monk to grow in virtue, so that though he engages in ascetic labours in the end he remains barren. For whether you are a beginner, or midway along the spiritual path, or have attained the stage of perfection, self-esteem always tries to insinuate itself, and it nullifies your efforts to live a holy life, so that you waste your time in listlessness and day-dreaming.

I have also learnt this from experience, that unless a monk cultivates the following virtues he will never make progress: fasting, self-control, keeping vigil, patient endurance, courage, stillness, prayer, silence, inward grief and humility. These virtues generate and protect each other. Constant fasting withers lust and begets self-control. Self-control enables us to keep vigils, vigils beget patient endurance, endurance courage, courage stillness, stillness prayer, prayer silence, silence inward grief, and grief begets humility. Or, going in the reverse order, you will find how daughters give birth to mothers—how, that is to say, humility begets inward grief, and so on. In the realm of the virtues there is nothing more important than this form of mutual generation. The things opposite to these virtues are obvious to all.

Here we should specify the toils and hardships of the ascetic life and explain clearly how we should embark on each task. We must do this lest someone who coasts along without exerting himself, simply relying on what he has heard, and who consequently remains barren, should blame us or other writers, alleging that things are not as we have said. For it is only through travail of heart and bodily toil that the work can properly be carried out. Through them the grace of the Holy Spirit is revealed. This is the grace with which we and all Christians are endowed at baptism but which through neglect of the commandments has been stifled by the passions. Now through God's ineffable mercy it awaits our repentance, so that at the end of our life we may not because of our barrenness hear the words "Take the talent from him," and "What he thinks he has will be taken away from him" (cf. Matt. 25:28–29), and may not be sent to hell to suffer endlessly in Gehenna. No activity, whether bodily or spiritual, unaccompanied by toil and hardship bears fruit; "for the kingdom of heaven is entered forcibly," says the Lord, "and those who force themselves take possession of it" (Matt. 11:12), where "forcibly" and "force" relate to the body's awareness of exertion in all things.

Many for long years may have been preoccupied with the spiritual life without exerting themselves, or may still be preoccupied with it in this way; but because they do not assiduously embrace hardships with heartfelt fervour and sense of purpose, and have repudiated the severity of bodily toil, they remain devoid of purity, without a share in the Holy Spirit. Those who practice the spiritual life, but do so carelessly and lazily, may think that they make considerable efforts; but they will never reap any harvest because they have not exerted themselves and basically have never experienced any real tribulation. A witness to this is St. John Klimakos, who says, "However exalted our way of life may be, it is worthless and bogus if our heart does not suffer." Sometimes when we fail to exert ourselves we are in our listlessness carried away by spurious forms of distraction and plunged into darkness, thinking we can find rest in them when that is impossible. The truth is that we are then bound invisibly by unloosable cords and become inert and ineffective in everything we do, for we grow increasingly sluggish, especially if we are beginners. For those who have reached the stage of perfection everything is profitable in moderation. St. Ephrem also testifies to this when he says, "Persistently suffer hardships in order to avoid the hardship of vain sufferings." For unless, to use the prophet's phrase, our loins are exhausted by the weakness induced through the exertions of fasting, and unless like a woman in childbirth we are afflicted with pains arising from the constriction of our heart, we will not conceive the Spirit of salvation in the earth of our heart (cf. Isa. 21:3; 26:18). Instead, all we will have to boast about is the many profitless years we have spent in the wilderness, lazily cultivating stillness and imagining that we are somebody. At the moment of our death we will all know for certain what is the outcome of our life.

No one can learn the art of virtue by himself, though some have taken experience as their teacher. For to act on one's own and not on the advice of those who have gone before us is overweening presumption—or, rather, it engenders such presumption. If the Son does nothing of His own accord, but does only what the Father has taught Him (cf. John 5:19–20), and the Spirit will not speak of His own accord (cf. John 16:3), who can think he has attained such heights of virtue that he does not need anyone to initiate him into the mysteries? Such a person is deluded and out of his mind rather than virtuous. One should therefore listen to those who have experienced the hardships involved in cultivating the virtues and should cultivate them as they have—that is to say, by severe fasting, painful self-control, steadfast vigils, laborious genuflexions, assiduous standing motionless, constant prayer, unfeigned humility, ceaseless contrition and compunctive sorrow, eloquent silence, as if seasoned with salt (cf. Col. 4:6), and by patience in all things. You must not be always relaxing or pray sitting down, before it is the proper time to do so, or before age or sickness compels you. For, as Scripture says, "You will nourish yourself on the hardships of your practice of the virtues" (cf. Ps. 128:2. LXX); and, "The kingdom of heaven is entered forcibly" (Matt. 11:12). Hence those who diligently strive day by day to practise the virtues that we have mentioned will with God's help gather in the harvest at the appropriate time.

Questions

1. Describe two techniques of prayer as set forth by St. Gregory of Sinai.
2. How does this text reflect the influence of other Eastern saints?
3. What are the various views regarding the role of psalmodizing in prayer?

St. Catherine of Siena

St. Catherine of Siena lived in Italy in the fourteenth century, a time when it must have been terribly easy to give up hope in God, the Church, and the world. Great plagues struck Europe at this time, killing those who dared to help their brothers and sisters in need. Equally terribly, the popes were under the sway of the French kings and had established an apparently permanent residence in Avignon rather than Rome. St. Catherine helped persuade the pope to return to Rome, but by the time she died at age thirty-three, the Great Schism had struck the papacy, due to confusion over legitimate succession. From this terrible period, St. Catherine emerges as one of the greatest theologians the Church has known. In her mystical *Dialogue* with God, she indicates the central role, in the life of prayer, of humility and focusing on God's goodness and mercy. Prayer sustains us in a life of dependence on God rather than dependence on our own works.

T HE SOUL, ONCE ON HER WAY, must cross over by way of the teaching of Christ crucified, truly loving virtue and hating vice. If she perseveres to the end she will come to the house of self-knowledge, where she shuts herself up in watching and continuous prayer, completely cut off from worldly company.

Excerpts from Catherine of Siena, *The Dialogue*, from The Classics of Western Spirituality, translation and introduction by Suzanne Noffke, O.P., 122–30. Copyright © 1980 by Paulist Press, Inc., New York/Mahwah, N.J. Used with permission of Paulist Press. www.paulistpress.com.

Why does she shut herself up? Through fear, because she knows how imperfect she is. And through her longing to attain a genuine and free love. She sees well that there is no other way to attain it, and so she waits with a lively faith for my coming, so that she may grow in grace.

How does one come to know lively faith? By persevering in virtue. You must never turn back for anything at all. You must not break away from holy prayer for any reason except obedience or charity. For often during the time scheduled for prayer the devil comes with all sorts of struggles and annoyances—even more than when you are not at prayer. He does this to make you weary of holy prayer. Often he will say, "This sort of prayer is worthless to you. You should not think about or pay attention to anything except vocal prayer." He makes it seem this way so that you will become weary and confused, and abandon the exercise of prayer. But prayer is a weapon with which you can defend yourself against every enemy. If you hold it with love's hand and the arm of free choice, this weapon, with the light of most holy faith, will be your defense.

Know, dearest daughter, that if she truly perseveres, the soul learns every virtue in constant and faithful humble prayer. Therefore she ought to persevere and never abandon it—neither for the devil's illusion, nor through her own weakness (that is, any thought or impulse within her own flesh), nor because of what others say. For often the devil will sit on their tongues and make them say things calculated to hinder her prayer. She must overcome them all with the virtue of perseverance.

Oh, how delightful to the soul and pleasing to me is holy prayer made in the house of self-knowledge and knowledge of me! The soul opens her mind's eye with the light of faith and with her affection steeped in the fullness of my charity made visible in the sight of my only-begotten Son, who showed it with his blood. That blood inebriates the soul. It clothes her in the fire of divine charity. It gives her the food of the sacrament that I have set up for you in the hostel of the mystic body of holy Church, the body and the blood of my Son, wholly God and wholly human, given to holy Church to be ministered by the hands of my vicar, who holds the key to this blood.

This is the hostel I had mentioned to you that stands on the bridge to dispense the food to strengthen the pilgrim travelers who go the way of my Truth's teaching, so that weakness will not cause them to fall.

This food gives more or less strength according to the desire of those who receive it, whether they receive it sacramentally or virtually. "Sacramentally" is when one communicates in the holy Sacrament. "Virtually" is communicating through holy desire, both in longing for communion and in esteem for the blood of Christ crucified. In other words, one is communicating sacramentally in the loving charity one finds and tastes in the blood because one sees that it was shed through love. And so the soul is inebriated and set on fire and sated with holy longing, finding herself filled completely with love of me and of her neighbors.

Where did the soul learn this? In the house of self-knowledge, in holy prayer. There she lost her imperfection, just as the disciples and Peter lost their imperfection and learned perfection by staying inside in watchful prayer. How? Through perseverance seasoned with most holy faith.

But do not think that such ardor and nourishment is to be had from vocal prayer alone, as many souls believe. Their prayer consists more in words than in affection, and they seem to be concerned only to complete their multitude of psalms and to say a great many Our Fathers. When they have finished the number they have set themselves to say, they seem to think of nothing more. It seems they place the whole purpose of prayer in what is said vocally. But that is not how they should act, for if that is all they do they will draw little fruit from it and will please me little.

But if you ask me whether one should abandon vocal prayer, since it seems not everyone is drawn to mental prayer, the answer is no. A person has to walk step by step. I know well that, because the soul is imperfect before she is perfect, her prayer is imperfect as well. She should certainly, while she is still imperfect, stay with vocal prayer so as not to fall into laziness, but she should not omit mental prayer. In other words, while she says the words she should make an effort to concentrate on my love, pondering at the same time her own sins and the blood of my only-begotten Son. There she will find the expansiveness of my charity and forgiveness for her sins. Thus self-knowledge and the consideration of her sins ought to bring her to know my goodness to her and make her continue her exercise in true humility.

Now I do not want her to think about her sins individually, lest her mind be contaminated by the memory of specific ugly sins. I mean that I do not want her to, nor should she, think about her sins either in general or specifically without calling to mind the blood and the greatness of my mercy. Otherwise she will only be confounded. For if self-knowledge and the thought of sin are not seasoned with remembrance of the blood and hope for mercy, the result is bound to be confusion. And along with this comes the devil, who under the guise of contrition and hatred for sin and sorrow for her guilt leads her to eternal damnation. Because of this— though not this alone—she would end in despair if she did not reach out for the arm of my mercy.

This is one of the subtle deceptions the devil works on my servants. So for your own good, to escape his deceit and to be pleasing to me, you must keep expanding your heart and your affection in the immeasurable greatness of my mercy, with true humility. For know this: The devil's pride cannot tolerate a humble mind, nor can his confounding withstand the greatness of my goodness and mercy when a soul is truly hopeful.

Do you recall when the devil wanted to frighten you with confusion? He tried to show you that your life was a delusion and that you had neither followed nor done my will. But you did what you should have done and what my goodness gave you strength to do—for my goodness is never hidden from anyone who wants to receive it. By my mercy and with humility you stood up and said, "I confess to my Creator that my life has been spent wholly in darkness. But I will hide myself in the wounds of Christ crucified and bathe in his blood, and so my wickedness will be consumed and I will rejoice with desire in my Creator."

You know that at this the devil fled. But he returned with another attack, wanting to exalt you in pride. He said, "You are perfect and pleasing to God. You no longer need to torture yourself or weep over your sins." But I gave you light and you saw the way you should take, that you should humble yourself. And you answered the devil, "How wretched I am! John the Baptist never sinned. He was made holy in his mother's womb, yet he did such great penance. But I have committed so many sins and have not yet even begun to acknowledge it with tears and true contrition, seeing who God is who is offended by me and who I am who offend him!"

Then the devil, unable to bear your humility of spirit and your trust in my goodness, said to you, "Damnable woman! There is no getting at you! If I throw you down in confusion you lift yourself up to mercy. If I exalt you you throw yourself down. You come even to hell in your humility, and even in hell you hound me. So I will not come back to you again, because you beat me with the cudgel of charity!"

The soul, then, should season her self-knowledge with knowledge of my goodness, and her knowledge of me with self-knowledge. In this way vocal prayer will profit the soul who practices it and it will please me. And if she perseveres in its practice, she will advance from imperfect vocal prayer to perfect mental prayer.

But if she looks only to the completion of her tally of prayers, or if she abandons mental prayer for vocal, she will never advance. A soul may set herself to say a certain number of oral prayers. But I may visit her spirit in one way or another, sometimes with a flash of self-knowledge and contrition for her sinfulness, sometimes in the greatness of my love setting before her mind the presence of my Truth in different ways, depending on my pleasure or her longings. And sometimes the soul will be so foolish as to abandon my visitation, which she senses within her spirit, in order to complete her tally. As if it were a matter of conscience to abandon what one has begun!

This is not the way she should act. If she did, she would be a dupe of the devil. No. As soon as she senses her spirit ready for my visitation, she ought to abandon vocal prayer. Then, after the mental prayer, if she has time, she can resume what she had set herself to say. If she does not have time she ought not worry or be annoyed or confounded in spirit. But the Divine Office is an exception to this. Clerics and religious are obliged to say it, and sin if they do not say it. They must say their Office right up to the time of death. If they feel their mind drawn by desire and lifted up at the time appointed for saying the Office, they should arrange to say it either earlier or later so they will not fail in their duty regarding the Office.

As far as concerns any other prayer the soul might begin, she ought to begin vocally as a way to reach mental prayer. When she senses that her spirit is ready she should abandon vocal prayer with this intent. Such prayer, made in the way I have told you, will bring her to perfection. This is why she should not abandon vocal prayer, whatever its form, but should advance step by step. Thus, with practice and perseverance she will experience prayer in truth and that food which is the body and blood of my only-begotten Son. And this is why I told you that some souls communicate in the body and blood of Christ actually, even though not sacramentally, when they communicate in loving charity, which they enjoy in holy prayer, in proportion to their desire.

A soul who walks with scant prudence and not step by step finds little. But one who has much finds much. For the more the soul tries to free her affection and bind it to me by the light of understanding, the more she will come to know. One who knows more loves more, and loving more, enjoys more.

You see, then, perfect prayer is achieved not with many words but with loving desire, when the soul rises up to me with knowledge of herself, each movement seasoned by the other. In this way she will have vocal and mental prayer at the same time, for the two stand together like the active life and the contemplative life. Still, vocal and mental prayer are understood in many different ways. This is why I told you that holy desire, that is, having a good and holy will, is continual prayer. This will and desire rises at the appointed time and place to add actual prayer to the continual prayer of holy desire. So also with vocal prayer. As long as the soul remains firm in holy desire and will, she will make it at the appointed time. But sometimes, beyond the appointed times, she makes this continual prayer, as charity asks of her for her neighbors' good and according to the need she sees and the situation in which I have placed her.

The principle of holy will means that each of you must work for the salvation of souls according to your own situation. Whatever you do in word or deed for the good of your neighbor is a real prayer. (I am assuming that you actually pray as such at the appointed time.) Apart from your prayers of obligation, however, everything you do can be a prayer, whether in itself or in the form of charity to your neighbors, because of the way you use the situation at hand. This is what my glorious trumpeter Paul said: "One who never stops doing good never stops praying." And this is why I told you that actual prayer can be one with mental prayer in many ways. For when actual prayer is done in the way I described, it is done with loving charity, and this loving charity is continual prayer.

Now I have told you how the soul arrives at mental prayer, that is, by practice and perseverance, and by abandoning vocal prayer for mental when I visit her. I have also told you about ordinary prayer, and ordinary vocal prayer apart from appointed times, and the prayer of a good and holy will, and prayer both in itself and in the form of [service to] your neighbors done with good will apart from the scheduled time for prayer.

Courageously, then, should the soul spur herself on with prayer as her mother. And this is what the soul does when she has attained the love of friendship and filial love, and shuts herself up in the house of self-knowledge. But if she does not keep to the paths I have described, she will stay forever lukewarm and imperfect, and will love only to the extent that she experiences profit and pleasure in me or in her neighbors.

In regard to this imperfect love I want to tell you—I will not remain silent—about how people can be deluded by thus loving me for their own consolation. And I want you to know that when my servants love me imperfectly, they love this consolation more than they love me.

Here is how you can recognize such imperfection: Watch people when they are deprived of either spiritual or material comfort. Take, for example, worldly people who sometimes act virtuously when they are prosperous, but if trouble comes (which I send for their own good) they are disturbed about what little bit of good they had been doing. If you were to ask them, "Why are you disturbed?" they would answer, "I seem to have lost what little bit of good I was doing. I no longer do it with the same heart and soul as I used to. And the reason is this trouble that has come my way. For it seems I did more before, and did it more peacefully, with a more quiet heart, than I do now." But it is their selfish pleasure that is deceiving them.

It is not true that trouble is the culprit, nor that they love less or are doing less. The works they do in time of trouble are worth as much in themselves as they were before in time of consolation. In fact, they could be worth more if these people had patience. But this comes about because their pleasure was in their prosperity. Then they loved me with a little bit of an act of virtue, and they pacified their spirit with that little bit of effort. And now when they are deprived of what they found contentment in, it seems to them that any contentment they had found in their efforts at all has been taken away, but that is not the case.

They are like a man in a garden who, because it gives him pleasure, finds contentment in working the garden. To him it seems his contentment is in the work, but his contentment is really in the pleasure the garden gives him. Here is how you can tell that he takes pleasure more in the garden than in the work: If the garden is taken away he feels bereft of pleasure. Now if his chief pleasure had been in his work, he would not have lost it, because one cannot be deprived of the practice of doing good unless one so chooses, even though prosperity may be taken away as the garden was taken away from this man.

These people, then, are deluded in their works by their own selfish passion. This is why they have the habit of saying, "I know I used to do better and had more consolation before I had this trouble than I do now.

It used to be worth doing good, but now there is no profit in it for me, nor the least bit of pleasure." Their perception and their words are both false. If their pleasure in doing good had come from love for the good that virtue is, they would never have lost it. In fact, their pleasure would have increased. But because their doing good was built on their own sensual well-being, pleasure failed them and fled.

This is how ordinary people are deluded in some of their good works. It is their very own selves, their selfish sensual pleasure, that deceives them.

But my servants, even though their love is still imperfect, seek and love me for love's sake rather than for the consolation and pleasure they find in me. Now I do reward every good deed—but the measure of the reward is the recipient's love. Thus I give spiritual consolation in prayer, now in one way, now in another. But it is not my intention that the soul should receive this consolation foolishly, paying more attention to my gift than to me. I want her to be more concerned about the loving charity with which I give it to her, and to her unworthiness to receive it, than to the pleasure of her own consolation. If she foolishly takes only the pleasure without considering my love for her, she will reap the sort of harm and delusion of which I am about to tell you.

First of all, because she is deluded by her own consolation, this is what she seeks and this is where she finds her pleasure. And more: When she has experienced my consolation and my visitation within her in one way, and then that way ceases, she goes back along the road by which she had come, hoping to find the same thing again. But I do not always give in the same way, lest it seem as if I had nothing else to give. No, I give in many ways, as it pleases my goodness and according to the soul's need. But in her foolishness she looks for my gift only in that one way, trying as it were to impose rules on the Holy Spirit.

That is not the way to act. Instead, she should cross courageously along the bridge of the teaching of Christ crucified and there receive my gifts when, where, and as my goodness pleases to give them. And if I hold back it is not out of hate but love, so that she may seek me in truth and love me not just for her pleasure, but humbly accept my charity more than any pleasure she may find. For if she does otherwise and runs only after pleasure in her own way rather than mine, she will experience pain and unbearable confusion when the object of her delight, as her mind sees it, seems to be taken away.

Such are those who choose consolation in their own way. Once they find pleasure in me in a given fashion, they want to go on with just that. Sometimes they are so foolish that if I visit them in any other way than that, they resist and do not accept it, still wanting only what they have imagined.

This is the fault of their selfish passion in the spiritual pleasure they found in me. But they are deluded. It would be impossible to be always the same. For the soul cannot stand still; she has either to advance toward virtue or turn back. In the same way the spirit cannot stand still in me in one pleasure without my goodness giving her more. And I give these gifts very differently: Sometimes I give the pleasure of a spiritual gladness; sometimes contrition and contempt for sin, which will make it seem as if the spirit is inwardly troubled. Sometimes I am in the soul without her sensing my presence. Sometimes I make my Truth, the incarnate Word, take shape before her mind's eye in different ways, and yet it will seem that in her feelings the soul does not sense him with the ardor and delight she thinks ought to follow on such a vision. And sometimes she will see nothing but will feel tremendous pleasure.

All this I do out of love, to support her and make her grow in the virtue of humility and in perseverance, and to teach her that she should not try to lay down rules for me and that her goal is not consolation but only virtue built on me. I want her to accept humbly, in season and out, with loving affection, the affection with which I give to her, and to believe with lively faith that I give as her welfare demands or as is needed to bring her to great perfection.

So she should remain humble. Her beginning and end should be in the love of my charity, and in this charity she should accept pleasure and its absence in terms of my will rather than her own. This is the way to avoid delusion and to receive all things in love from me, for I am their end and they are grounded in my gentle will.

Questions

1. Why must we schedule time for prayer?
2. How is perfect prayer achieved?
3. What is the relationship between vocal prayer and mental prayer?

St. Ignatius of Loyola

Born in Spain in 1491, St. Ignatius of Loyola died in Rome in 1556 as the founder of the Society of Jesus (Jesuits). He spent much of his boyhood and all of his twenties as a courtier and soldier. While defending the castle of Pamplona against the forces of King Francis I of France, Ignatius was wounded in both legs; his conversion occurred during his convalescence. In 1522, he began travels intended to take him to the Holy Land, but hostilities with the Ottoman Empire prevented him from reaching the Holy Land, and he instead spent the next eleven years (1524–1535) studying philosophy and theology at Barcelona, Alcalá, Salamanca, and Paris. On August 15, 1534, having received the Master of Arts in theology at Paris, he took a vow of poverty and chastity with companions such as St. Francis Xavier. In 1540, the Society of Jesus was formally approved by Pope Paul III. The following excerpt comes from his renowned *Spiritual Exercises*, composed and refined btween 1522 and 1541. St. Ignatius explains the purposes of the four weeks of the Retreat and gives advice on how to administer the exercises so that retreatants, from various walks of life, will be drawn closer to God.

Excerpts from *Ignatius of Loyola: The Spiritual Exercises and Selected Works*, from The Classics of Western Spirituality, edited by George E. Ganss, S.J., 121–28. Copyright © 1991 by George E. Ganss, S.J., Paulist Press, Inc., New York/ Mahwah, N.J. Used with permission of Paulist Press. www.paulistpress.com.

IHS
Introductory Explanations, to Gain
Some Understanding of the Spiritual Exercises which Follow, and to
Aid Both the One Who Gives Them and the One Who Receives Them

The First Explanation. By the term Spiritual Exercises we mean every method of examination of conscience, meditation, contemplation, vocal or mental prayer, and other spiritual activities, such as will be mentioned later. For, just as taking a walk, traveling on foot, and running are physical exercises, so is the name of spiritual exercises given to any means of preparing and disposing our soul to rid itself of all its disordered affections and then, after their removal, of seeking and finding God's will in the ordering of our life for the salvation of our soul.

The Second. The person who gives to another the method and procedure for meditation or contemplating should accurately narrate the history contained in the contemplation or meditation, going over the points with only a brief or summary explanation. For in this way the person who is contemplating, by taking this history as the authentic foundation, and by going over it and reasoning about it for oneself, can thus discover something that will bring better understanding or a more personalized concept of the history—either through one's own reasoning or to the extent that the understanding is enlightened by God's grace. This brings more spiritual relish and spiritual fruit than if the one giving the Exercises had lengthily explained and amplified the meaning of the history. For, what fills and satisfies the soul consists, not in knowing much, but in our understanding the realities profoundly and in savoring them interiorly.

The Third. In all the following Spiritual Exercises we use the acts of the intellect in reasoning and of the will in eliciting acts of the affections. In regard to the affective acts which spring from the will we should note that when we are conversing with God our Lord or his saints vocally or mentally, greater reverence is demanded of us than when we are using the intellect to understand.

The Fourth. Four Weeks are taken for the following Exercises, corresponding to the four parts into which they are divided. That is, the First Week is devoted to the consideration and contemplation of sins; the Second, to the life of Christ our Lord up to and including Palm Sunday; the Third, to the Passion of Christ our Lord; and the Fourth, to the Resurrection and Ascension. To this week are appended the Three Methods of Praying. However, this does not mean that each week must necessarily consist of seven or eight days. During the First Week some persons happen to be slower in finding what they are seeking, that is, contrition, sorrow, and tears for their sins. Similarly, some persons work more diligently than others, and are more pushed back and forth and probed for different spirits. In some cases, therefore, the week needs to be shortened, and in others lengthened. This holds as well for all the following weeks, while the retreatant is seeking for what corresponds to their subject matter. But the Exercises ought to be completed in thirty days, more or less.

The Fifth. The persons who receive the Exercises will benefit greatly by entering upon them with great spirit and generosity toward their Creator and Lord, and by offering all their desires and freedom to him so that his Divine Majesty can make use of their persons and of all they possess in whatsoever way is according to his most holy will.

The Sixth. When the one giving the Exercises notices that the person making them is not experiencing any spiritual motions in his or her soul, such as consolations or desolations, or is not being moved one way or another by different spirits, the director should question the exercitant much about the Exercises: Whether the exercitant is making them at the appointed times, how they are being made, and whether the Additional Directives are being diligently observed. The director should ask about each of these items in particular. . . .

The Seventh. When the giver of the Exercises sees that the recipient is experiencing desolation and temptation, he or she should not treat the retreatant severely or harshly, but gently and kindly. The director should encourage and strengthen the exercitant for the future, unmask the deceptive tactics of the enemy of our human nature, and help the retreatant to prepare and dispose himself or herself for the consolation which will come.

The Eighth. According to the need perceived in the recipient with respect to the desolations and deceptive tactics of the enemy, and also the consolations, the giver of the Exercises may explain to the retreatant the rules of the First and Second Weeks for recognizing the different kinds of spirits. . . .

The Ninth. This point should be noticed. When an exercitant spiritually inexperienced is going through the First Week of the Exercises he or she may be tempted grossly and openly, for example, by being shown obstacles to going forward in the service of God our Lord, in the form of hardships, shame, fear about worldly honor, and the like. In such a case the one giving the Exercises should not explain to this retreatant the rules on different kinds of spirits for the Second Week. For to the same extent that the rules of the First Week will help him or her, those of the Second Week will be harmful. They are too subtle and advanced for such a one to understand.

The Tenth. When the one giving the Exercises perceives that the recipient is being assailed and tempted under the appearance of good, the proper time has come to explain to the retreatant the rules of the Second Week mentioned just above. For ordinarily the enemy of human nature tempts under the appearance of good more often when a person is performing the Exercises in the illuminative life, which corresponds to the Exercises of the Second Week, than in the purgative life, which corresponds to those of the First Week.

The Eleventh. It is helpful for a person receiving the Exercises of the First Week to know nothing about what is to be done in the Second, but to work diligently during the First Week at obtaining what he or she is seeking, just as if there were no anticipation of finding anything good in the Second.

The Twelfth. The one giving the Exercises should insist strongly with the person receiving them that he or she should remain for a full hour in each of the five Exercises of contemplation which will be made each day; and further, that the recipient should make sure always to have the satisfaction of knowing that a full hour was spent on the exercise—indeed, more rather than less. For the enemy usually exerts special efforts to get a person to shorten the hour of contemplation, meditation or prayer.

The Thirteenth. This too should be noted. In time of consolation it is easy and scarcely taxing to remain in contemplation for a full hour, but during desolation it is very hard to fill out the time. Hence, to act against the desolation and overcome the temptations, the exercitant ought to remain always a little longer than the full hour, and in this way become accustomed not merely to resist the enemy but even to defeat him.

The Fourteenth. If the one giving the Exercises sees that the exercitant is proceeding with consolation and great fervor, he or she should warn the person not to make some promise or vow which is unconsidered or hasty. The more unstable the director sees the exercitant to be, the more earnest should be the forewarning and caution. For although it is altogether right for someone to advise another to enter religious life, which entails the taking of vows of obedience, poverty, and chastity; and although a good work done under a vow is more meritorious than one done without it; still one ought to bestow much thought on the circumstances and character of each person, and on the helps or hindrances one is likely to meet with in carrying out what one wishes to promise.

The Fifteenth. The one giving the Exercises should not urge the one receiving them toward poverty or any other promise more than toward their opposites, or to one state or way of life more than to another. Outside the Exercises it is lawful and meritorious for us to counsel those who are probably suitable for it to choose continence, virginity, religious life, and all forms of evangelical perfection. But during these Spiritual Exercises when a person is seeking God's will, it is more appropriate and far better that the Creator and Lord himself should communicate himself to the devout soul, embracing it with love, inciting it to praise of himself, and disposing it for the way which will most enable the soul to serve him in the future. Accordingly, the one giving the Exercises ought not to lean or incline in either direction but rather, while standing by like the pointer of a scale in equilibrium, to allow the Creator to deal immediately with the creature and the creature with its Creator and Lord.

The Sixteenth. For this purpose—namely, that the Creator and Lord may with greater certainty be the one working in his creature—if by chance the exercitant feels an affection or inclination to something in a disordered way, it is profitable for that person to strive with all possible effort to come over to the opposite of that to which he or she is wrongly attached. Thus, if someone is inclined to pursue and hold on to an office or benefice, not for the honor and glory of God our Lord or for the spiritual welfare of souls, but rather for one's own temporal advantages and interests, one should try to bring oneself to desire the opposite. One should make earnest prayers and other spiritual exercises and ask God our Lord for the contrary; that is, to have no desire for this office or benefice or anything else unless his Divine Majesty has put proper order into those desires, and has by this means so changed one's earlier attachment that one's motive in desiring or holding on to one thing rather than another will now be only the service, honor, and glory of his Divine Majesty.

The Seventeenth. Although the one giving the Exercises should not endeavor to ask about or know the personal thoughts or sins of the exercitant, it is very advantageous for the director to be faithfully informed about the various agitations and thoughts which the different spirits stir up in the retreatant. For then, in accordance with the person's greater or lesser progress, the director will be able to communicate spiritual exercises adapted to the needs of the person who is agitated in this way.

The Eighteenth. The Spiritual Exercises should be adapted to the disposition of the persons who desire to make them, that is, to their age, education, and ability. In this way someone who is uneducated or has a weak constitution will not be given things he or she cannot well bear or profit from without fatigue.

Similarly exercitants should be given, each one, as much as they are willing to dispose themselves to receive, for their greater help and progress.

Consequently, a person who wants help to get some instruction and reach a certain level of peace of soul can be given the Particular Examen, and then the General Examen, and farther, the Method of Praying for a half hour in the morning on the Commandments, the Capital Sins, and other such procedures. Such a person can also be encouraged to weekly confession of sins and, if possible, to reception of the Eucharist every two weeks or, if better disposed, weekly. This procedure is more appropriate for persons who are rather simple or illiterate. They should be given an explanation of each of the commandments, the seven capital sins, the precepts of the Church, the five senses, and the works of mercy.

Likewise, if the one giving the Exercises sees that the recipient is a person poorly qualified or of little natural capacity from whom much fruit is not to be expected, it is preferable to give to such a one some of these light Exercises until he or she has confessed, and then to give ways of examining one's conscience and a program for confession more frequent than before, that the person may preserve what has been acquired. But this should be done without going on to matters pertaining to the Election or to other Exercises beyond the First Week. This is especially the case when there are others with whom greater results can be achieved and time is insufficient to do everything.

The Nineteenth. A person who is involved in public affairs or pressing occupations but educated or intelligent may take an hour and a half each day to perform the Exercises. To such a one the director can explain the end for which human beings are created. Then he or she can explain for half an hour the Particular Examen, then the General Examen, and the method of confessing and receiving the Eucharist. For three days this exercitant should make a meditation for an hour each morning on the first, second, and third sins; then for another three days at the same hour the meditation on the court-record of one's own sins; then for a further three days at the same hour the meditation on the punishment corresponding to sins. During these three meditations the ten Additional Directives should be given the exercitant. For the mysteries of Christ our Lord this exercitant should follow the same procedure as is explained below and at length throughout the Exercises themselves.

The Twentieth. A person who is more disengaged, and who desires to make all the progress possible, should be given all the Spiritual Exercises in the same sequence in which they proceed below. Ordinarily, in making them an exercitant will achieve more progress the more he or she withdraws from all friends and acquaintances, and from all earthly concerns; for example, by moving out of one's place of residence and taking a different house or room where one can live in the greatest possible solitude, and thus be free to attend Mass and Vespers daily without fear of hindrance from acquaintances. Three principal advantages flow from this seclusion, among many others.

First, by withdrawing from friends and acquaintances and likewise from various activities that are not well ordered, in order to serve and praise God our Lord, we gain much merit in the eyes of his Divine Majesty.

Second, by being secluded in this way and not having our mind divided among many matters, but by concentrating instead all our attention on one alone, namely, the service of our Creator and our own spiritual progress, we enjoy a freer use of our natural faculties for seeking diligently what we so ardently desire.

Third, the more we keep ourselves alone and secluded, the more fit do we make ourselves to approach and attain to our Creator and Lord; and the nearer we come to him in this way, the more do we dispose ourselves to receive graces and gifts from his divine and supreme goodness.

Questions

1. What is a "spiritual exercise"?
2. How must the one giving the Exercises be sensitive to the condition of the exercitant?
3. Why is contemplation so important in discerning God's will?

St. Teresa of Avila

St. Teresa of Avila (1515–1582) was born into a devout family. In 1535, she entered the Carmelite Monastery of the Incarnation at Avila. For the next four years she endured a serious illness. In the following decades, she experienced a profound conversion and mystical raptures and visions. In 1560, she began her reform Carmelite movement, an effort to develop a stricter religious observance, in which she was assisted by St. John of the Cross, among others. Her last years were devoted to founding new convents throughout Spain as the reform spread. The following selection from *The Interior Castle* describes spiritual marriage with God through contemplative union.

The Seventh Dwelling Place

Chapter 1

YOU WILL THINK, SISTERS, that since so much has been said about this spiritual path it will be impossible for anything more to be said.

From *The Collected Works of St. Teresa of Avila*, vol. 2, translated by Kieran Kavanaugh and Otilio Rodriguez, 427–43. Copyright © 1980 by Washington Province of Discalced Carmelites, ICS Publications, 2131 Lincoln Road, N.E., Washington, DC, 20002-1199 U.S.A. www.icspublications.org.

Such a thought would be very foolish. Since the greatness of God is without limits, His works are too. Who will finish telling of His mercies and grandeurs? To do so is impossible, and thus do not be surprised at what was said, and will be said, because it is but a naught in comparison to what there is to tell of God. He grants us a great favor in having communicated these things to a person through whom we can know about them. Thus the more we know about His communication to creatures the more we will praise His grandeur and make the effort to have esteem for souls in which the Lord delights so much. Each one of us has a soul, but since we do not prize souls as is deserved by creatures made in the image of God we do not understand the deep secrets that lie in them.

May it please His Majesty, if He may thereby be served, to move my pen and give me understanding of how I might say something about the many things to be said and which God reveals to the one whom He places in this dwelling place. I have earnestly begged this of His Majesty since He knows that my intention is to make known His mercies that His name may be more praised and glorified.

I hope, not for myself but for you, Sisters, that He may grant me this favor. Thus you will understand how important it is for you not to impede your Spouse's celebration of this spiritual marriage with your souls, since this marriage brings so many blessings, as you will see. O great God! It seems that a creature as miserable as I should tremble to deal with a thing so foreign to what I deserve to understand. And, indeed, I have been covered with confusion wondering if it might not be better to conclude my discussion of this dwelling place with just a few words. For it seems to me that others will think I know about it through experience. This makes me extremely ashamed; for, knowing what I am, such a thought is a terrible thing. On the other hand, the thought of neglecting to explain this dwelling place seemed to me to be a temptation and weakness on my part, no matter how many of the above judgments you make about me. May God be praised and understood a little more, and let all the world cry out against me; how much more so in that I will perhaps be dead when what I write is seen. May He be blessed who lives, and will live, forever, amen.

When our Lord is pleased to have pity on this soul that He has already taken spiritually as His Spouse because of what it suffers and has suffered through its desires, He brings it, before the spiritual marriage is consummated, into His dwelling place which is this seventh. For just as in heaven so in the soul His Majesty must have a room where He dwells alone. Let us call it another heaven. It's very important for us, Sisters, not to think the soul is something dark. Since we do not see the soul, it usually seems that there is no such thing as interior light but only the exterior light which we all see, and that a certain darkness is in our soul. As for the soul that is not in grace, I confess this is so, but not through any fault of the Sun of Justice who dwells within it giving it being but because such a soul is incapable of receiving the light, as I believe I have said in the first dwelling place, according to what a certain person understood. For these unfortunate souls are as though in a dark prison, bound hands and feet, in regard to doing anything good that would enable them to merit, and blind and deaf. We can rightly take pity on them and reflect that at one time we were ourselves in this condition and that the Lord can also have mercy on them.

Let us take special care, Sisters, to beg this mercy of Him and not be careless, for it is a most generous alms to pray for those who are in mortal sin. Suppose we were to see a Christian with his hands fastened behind his back by a strong chain, bound to a post, and dying of hunger, not because of lack of food, for there are very choice dishes beside him, but because he cannot take hold of the food and eat, and even has great loathing for it; and suppose he sees that he is about to breathe his last and die, not just an earthly death but an eternal one. Wouldn't it be a terrible cruelty to stand looking at him and not feed him? Well, then, what if through your prayer the chains could be loosed? The answer is obvious. For the love of God I ask you always to remember in your prayers souls in mortal sin.

We are not speaking about them now but about those who already by the mercy of God have done penance for their sins and are in the state of grace. Thus we are not reflecting on something restricted to a corner but on an interior world where there is room for so many and such attractive dwelling places, as you have seen; and indeed it is right that the soul be like this since within it there is a dwelling place for God. Now then, when His Majesty is pleased to grant the soul this divine marriage that was mentioned, He first brings it into His own dwelling place. He desires that the favor be different from what it was at other times when He gave the soul raptures. I really believe that in rapture He unites it with Himself, as well as in the prayer of union that was mentioned. But it doesn't seem to the soul that it is called to enter into its center, as it is here in this dwelling place, but called to the superior part. These things matter little; whether the experience comes in one way or another, the Lord joins the soul to Himself. But He does so by making it blind and deaf, as was St. Paul in his conversion, and by taking away perception of the nature and kind of favor enjoyed, for the great delight the soul then feels is to see itself near God. Yet when He joins it to Himself, it doesn't understand anything; for all the faculties are lost.

In this seventh dwelling place the union comes about in a different way: our good God now desires to remove the scales from the soul's eyes and let it see and understand, although in a strange way, something of the favor He grants it. When the soul is brought into that dwelling place, the Most Blessed Trinity, all three Persons, through an intellectual vision, is revealed to it through a certain representation of the truth. First there comes an enkindling in the spirit in the manner of a cloud of magnificent splendor; and these Persons are distinct, and through an admirable knowledge the soul understands as a most profound truth that all three Persons are one substance and one power and one knowledge and one God alone. It knows in such a way that what we hold by faith, it understands, we can say, through sight—although the sight is not with the bodily eyes nor with the eyes of the soul, because we are not dealing with an imaginative vision. Here all three Persons communicate themselves to it, speak to it, and explain those words of the Lord in the Gospel: that He and the Father and the Holy Spirit will come to dwell with the soul that loves Him and keeps His commandments.

Oh, God help me! How different is hearing and believing these words from understanding their truth in this way! Each day this soul becomes more amazed, for these Persons never seem to leave it any more, but it clearly beholds, in the way that was mentioned, that they are within it. In the extreme interior, in some place very deep within itself, the nature of which it doesn't know how to explain, because of a lack of learning, it perceives this divine company.

You may think that as a result the soul will be outside itself and so absorbed that it will be unable to be occupied with anything else. On the contrary, the soul is much more occupied than before with everything pertaining to the service of God; and once its duties are over it remains with that enjoyable company. If the soul does not fail God, He will never fail, in my opinion, to make His presence clearly known to it. It has strong confidence that since God has granted this favor He will not allow it to lose the favor. Though the soul thinks this, it goes about with greater care than ever not to displease Him in anything.

It should be understood that this presence is not felt so fully, I mean so clearly, as when revealed the first time or at other times when God grants the soul this gift. For if the presence were felt so clearly, the soul would find it impossible to be engaged in anything else or even to live among people. But even though the presence is not perceived with this very clear light, the soul finds itself in this company every time it takes notice. Let's say that the experience resembles that of a person who after being in a bright room with others finds himself, once the shutters are closed, in darkness. The light by which he could see them is taken away. Until it returns he doesn't see them, but not for that reason does he stop knowing they are present. It might be asked whether the soul can see them when it so desires and the light returns. To see them does not lie in its power, but depends on when our Lord desires that the window of the intellect be opened. Great is the mercy He shows in never departing from the soul and in desiring that it perceive Him so manifestly.

It seems that the divine Majesty desires, through this wonderful company, to prepare the soul for more. Clearly, the soul will be truly helped in every way to advance in perfection and to lose the fear it sometimes had of the other favors He granted it, as was said. Such was the experience of this person, for in everything she found herself improved, and it seemed to her, despite the trials she underwent and the business affairs she had to attend to, that the essential part of her soul never moved from that room. As a result, it seemed to her that there was, in a certain way, a division in her soul. And while suffering some great trials a little after God granted her this favor, she complained of that part of the soul, as Martha complained of Mary, and sometimes pointed out that it was there always enjoying that quietude at its own pleasure while leaving her in the midst of so many trials and occupations that she could not keep it company.

This will seem to you, daughters, to be foolishness, but it truly happens in this way. Although we know that the soul is all one, what I say is no mere fancy; the experience is very common. Wherefore I said that interior things are seen in such a way that one understands with certitude that there is some kind of difference, a difference clearly recognized, between the soul and the spirit, even though they are both one. So delicate a division is perceived that sometimes it seems the one functions differently from the other, and so does the savor the Lord desires to give them seem different. It also seems to me that the soul and the faculties are not one but different. There are so many and such delicate things in the interior that it would be boldness on my part to set out to explain them. In heaven we will see all this, if the Lord in His mercy grants us the favor of bringing us there where we shall understand these secrets.

Chapter 2

Now then let us deal with the divine and spiritual marriage, although this great favor does not come to its perfect fullness as long as we live; for if we were to withdraw from God, this remarkable blessing would be lost.

The first time the favor is granted, His Majesty desires to show Himself to the soul through an imaginative vision of His most sacred humanity so that the soul will understand and not be ignorant of receiving this sovereign gift. With other persons the favor will be received in another form. With regard to the one of whom we are speaking, the Lord represented Himself to her, just after she had received Communion, in the form of shining splendor, beauty, and majesty, as He was after His resurrection, and told her that now it was time that she consider as her own what belonged to Him and that He would take care of what was hers, and He spoke other words destined more to be heard than to be mentioned.

It may seem that this experience was nothing new since at other times the Lord had represented Himself to the soul in such a way. The experience was so different that it left her indeed stupefied and frightened: first, because this vision came with great force; second, because of the words the Lord spoke to her; and also because in the interior of her soul, where He represented Himself to her, she had not seen other visions except the former one. You must understand that there is the greatest difference between all the previous visions and those of this dwelling place.

Between the spiritual betrothal and the spiritual marriage the difference is as great as that which exists between two who are betrothed and two who can no longer be separated.

I have already said that even though these comparisons are used, because there are no others better suited to our purpose, it should be understood that in this state there is no more thought of the body than if the soul were not in it, but one's thought is only of the spirit. In the spiritual marriage, there is still much less remembrance of the body because this secret union takes place in the very interior center of the soul, which must be where God Himself is, and in my opinion there is no need of any door for Him to enter. I say there is no need of any door because everything that has been said up until now seems to take place by means of the senses and faculties, and this appearance of the humanity of the Lord must also. But that which comes to pass in the union of the spiritual marriage is very different. The Lord appears in this center of the soul, not in an imaginative vision but in an intellectual one, although more delicate than those mentioned, as He appeared to the apostles without entering through the door when He said to them *pax vobis*. What God communicates here to the soul in an instant is a secret so great and a favor so sublime—and the delight the soul experiences so extreme—that I don't know what to compare it to. I can say only that the Lord wishes to reveal for that moment, in a more sublime manner than through any spiritual vision or taste, the glory of heaven. One can say no more—insofar as can be understood—than that the soul, I mean the spirit, is made one with God. For since His Majesty is also spirit, He has wished to show His love for us by giving some persons understanding of the point to which this love reaches so that we might praise His grandeur. For He has desired to be so joined with the creature that, just as those who are married cannot be separated, He doesn't want to be separated from the soul.

The spiritual betrothal is different, for the two often separate. And the union is also different because, even though it is the joining of two things into one, in the end the two can be separated and each remains by itself. We observe this ordinarily, for the favor of union with the Lord passes quickly, and afterward the soul remains without that company; I mean, without awareness of it. In this other favor from the Lord, no. The soul always remains with its God in that center. Let us say that the union is like the joining of two wax candles to such an extent that the flame coming from them is but one, or that the wick, the flame, and the wax are all one. But afterward one candle can be easily separated from the other and there are two candles; the same holds for the wick. In the spiritual marriage the union is like what we have when rain falls from the sky into a river or fount; all is water, for the rain that fell from heaven cannot be divided or separated from the water of the river. Or it is like what we have when a little stream enters the sea, there is no means of separating the two. Or, like the bright light entering a room through two different windows; although the streams of light are separate when entering the room, they become one.

Perhaps this is what St. Paul means in saying *He that is joined or united to the Lord becomes one spirit with him*, and is referring to this sovereign marriage, presupposing that His Majesty has brought the soul to it through union. And he also says: *For me to live is Christ, and to die is gain*. The soul as well, I think, can say these words now because this state is the place where the little butterfly we mentioned dies, and with the greatest joy because its life is now Christ.

And that its life is Christ is understood better, with the passing of time, by the effects this life has. Through some secret aspirations the soul understands clearly that it is God who gives life to our soul. These aspirations come very, very often in such a living way that they can in no way be doubted. The soul feels them very clearly even though they are indescribable. But the feeling is so powerful that sometimes the soul cannot avoid the loving expressions they cause, such as: O Life of my life! Sustenance that sustains me! and things of this sort. For from those divine breasts where it seems God is always sustaining the soul there flow streams of milk bringing comfort to all the people of the castle. It seems the Lord desires that in some manner these others in the castle may enjoy the great deal the soul is enjoying and that from that full-flowing river, where this tiny fount is swallowed up, a spurt of that water will sometimes be directed toward the sustenance of those who in corporeal things must serve these two who are wed. Just as a distracted person would feel this water if he were suddenly bathed in it, and would be unable to avoid feeling it, so are these operations recognized, and even with greater certitude. For just as a great gush of water could not reach us if it didn't have a source, as I have said, so it is understood clearly that there is Someone in the interior depths who shoots these arrows and gives life to this life, and that there is a Sun in the interior of the soul from which a brilliant light proceeds and is sent to the faculties. The soul, as I have said, does not move from that center nor is its peace lost; for the very One who gave peace to the apostles when they were together can give it to the soul.

It has occurred to me that this greeting of the Lord must have amounted to much more than is apparent from its sound. So, too, with the Lord's words to the glorious Magdalene that she go in peace. Since His words are effected in us as deeds, they must have worked in such a manner in those souls already disposed that everything corporeal in the soul was taken away and it was left in pure spirit. Thus the soul could be joined in this heavenly union with the uncreated Spirit. For it is very certain that in emptying ourselves of all that is creature and detaching ourselves from it for the love of God, the same Lord will fill us with Himself. And thus, while Jesus our Lord was once praying for His apostles—I don't remember where—He said that they were one with the Father and with Him, just as Jesus Christ our Lord is in the Father and the Father is in Him. I don't know what greater love there can be than this. And all of us are included here, for His Majesty said: *I ask not only for them but for all those who also will believe in me*; and He says: *I am in them.*

Oh, God help me, how true these words are! And how well they are understood by the soul who is in this prayer and sees for itself. How well we would all understand them if it were not for our own fault, since the words of Jesus Christ, our King and Lord, cannot fail. But since we fail by not disposing ourselves and turning away from all that can hinder this light, we do not see ourselves in this mirror that we contemplate, where our image is engraved.

Well, to return to what we were saying. The Lord puts the soul in this dwelling of His, which is the center of the soul itself. They say that the empyreal heaven where the Lord is does not move as do the other heavens; similarly, it seems, in the soul that enters here there are none of those movements that usually take place in the faculties and the imagination and do harm to the soul, nor do these stirrings take away its peace.

It seems I'm saying that when the soul reaches this state in which God grants it this favor, it is sure of its salvation and safe from falling again. I do not say such a thing, and wherever I so speak that it seems the soul is secure, this should be taken to mean as long as the divine Majesty keeps it in His hand and it does not offend Him. At least I know certainly that the soul doesn't consider itself safe even though it sees itself in this state and the state has lasted for some years. But it goes about with much greater fear than before, guarding itself from any small offense against God and with the strongest desires to serve Him, as will be said further on, and with habitual pain and confusion at seeing the little it can do and the great deal to which it is obliged. This pain is no small cross but a very great penance. For when this soul does penance, the delight will be greater in the measure that the penance is greater. The true penance comes when God takes away the soul's health and strength for doing penance. Even though I have mentioned elsewhere the great pain this lack causes, the pain is much more intense here. All these things must come to the soul from its roots, from where it is planted. The tree that is beside the running water is fresher and gives more fruit. What is there, then, to marvel at in the desires this soul has since its true spirit has become one with the heavenly water we mentioned?

Now then, to return to what I was saying, it should not be thought that the faculties, senses, and passions are always in this peace; the soul is, yes. But in those other dwelling places, times of war, trial, and fatigue are never lacking; however, they are such that they do not take the soul from its place and its peace; that is, as a rule.

This center of our soul, or this spirit, is something so difficult to explain, and even believe in, that I think, Sisters, I'll not give you the temptation to disbelieve what I say, for I do not know how to explain this center. That there are trials and sufferings and that at the same time the soul is in peace is a difficult thing to explain. I want to make one or more comparisons for you. Please God, I may be saying something through them; but if not, I know that I'm speaking the truth in what I say.

The King is in His palace and there are many wars in his kingdom and many painful things going on, but not on that account does he fail to be at his post. So here, even though in those other dwelling places there is much tumult and there are many poisonous creatures and the noise is heard, no one enters that center dwelling place and makes the soul leave. Nor do the things the soul hears make it leave; even though they cause it some pain, the suffering is not such as to disturb it and take away its peace. The passions are now conquered and have a fear of entering the center because they would go away from there more subdued.

Our entire body may ache; but if the head is sound, the head will not ache just because the body aches.

I am laughing to myself over these comparisons for they do not satisfy me, but I don't know any others. You may think what you want; what I have said is true.

Chapter 3

Now, then, we are saying that this little butterfly has already died, with supreme happiness for having found repose and because Christ lives in it. Let us see what life it lives, or how this life differs from the life it was living. For from the effects, we shall see if what was said is true. By what I can understand these effects are the following.

The first effect is a forgetfulness of self, for truly the soul, seemingly, no longer is, as was said. Everything is such that this soul doesn't know or recall that there will be heaven or life or honor for it, because it employs all it has in procuring the honor of God. It seems the words His Majesty spoke to her produced the deed in her. They were that she look after what is His and that He would look after what is hers. Thus, the soul doesn't worry about all that can happen. It experiences strange forgetfulness, for, as I say, seemingly the soul no longer is or would want to be anything in anything, except when it understands that there can come from itself something by which the glory and honor of God may increase even one degree. For this purpose the soul would very willingly lay down its life.

Don't think by this, daughters, that a person fails to remember to eat and sleep—doing so is no small torment—and to do all that he is obliged to in conformity with his state in life. We are speaking of interior matters, for there is little to say about exterior works. Rather, the soul's pain lies in seeing that what it can now do by its own efforts amounts to nothing. For no earthly thing would it fail to do all it can and understands to be of the service of our Lord.

The second effect is that the soul has a great desire to suffer, but not the kind of desire that disturbs it as previously. For the desire left in these souls that the will of God be done in them reaches such an extreme that they think everything His Majesty does is good. If He desires the soul to suffer, well and good; if not, it doesn't kill itself as it used to.

These souls also have a deep interior joy when they are persecuted, with much more peace than that mentioned, and without any hostile feelings toward those who do, or desire to do, them evil. On the contrary, such a soul gains a particular love for its persecutors, in such a way that if it sees these latter in some trial it feels compassion and would take on any burden to free them from their trial, and eagerly recommends them to God and would rejoice to lose the favors His Majesty grants it if He would bestow these same gifts on those others so that they wouldn't offend our Lord.

You have already seen the trials and afflictions these souls have experienced in order to die so as to enjoy our Lord. What surprises me most of all now is that they have just as great a desire to serve Him and that through them He be praised and that they may benefit some soul if they can. For not only do they not desire to die but they desire to live very many years suffering the greatest trials if through these they can help that the Lord be praised, even though in something very small. If they knew for certain that in leaving the body the soul would enjoy God, they wouldn't pay attention to that; nor do they think of the glory of the saints. They do not desire at that time to be in glory. Their glory lies in being able some way to help the Crucified, especially when they see He is so offended and that few there are who, detached from everything else, really look after His honor.

It is true that sometimes these things are forgotten, and the loving desires to enjoy God and leave this exile return, especially when the soul sees how little it serves Him. But soon it turns and looks within itself and at how continually it experiences His presence, and with that it is content and offers His Majesty the desire to live as the most costly offering it can give Him.

It has no more fear of death than it would of a gentle rapture. The fact is that He who gave those desires that were so excessive a torment, now gives these others. May He be always blessed and praised.

The desires these souls have are no longer for consolations or spiritual delight, since the Lord Himself is present with these souls and it is His Majesty who now lives. Clearly, His life was nothing but a continual torment, and He makes ours the same; at least with the desires, for in other things He leads us as the weak, although souls share much in His fortitude when He sees they have need of it.

There is a great detachment from everything and a desire to be always either alone or occupied in something that will benefit some soul. There are no interior trials or feelings of dryness, but the soul lives with a remembrance and tender love of our Lord. It would never want to go without praising Him. When it becomes distracted the Lord Himself awakens it in the manner mentioned, for one sees most clearly that that impulse, or I don't know what to call the feeling, proceeds from the interior depths of the soul, as was said of the impulses in the previous dwelling place. Here, in this dwelling place, these impulses are experienced most gently, but they do not proceed from the mind or the memory, nor do they come from anything that would make one think the soul did something on its own. This experience is an ordinary and frequent one, for it has been observed carefully. Just as a fire does not shoot its flames downward but upward, however great a fire is enkindled, so one experiences here that this interior movement proceeds from the center of the soul and awakens the faculties.

Certainly, if there were no other gain in this way of prayer except to understand the particular care God has in communicating with us and beseeching us to remain with Him—for this experience doesn't seem to be anything else—it seems to me that all the trials endured for the sake of enjoying these touches of His love, so gentle and penetrating, would be well worthwhile.

This you will have experienced, Sisters. For I think that when one has reached the prayer of union the Lord goes about with this concern if we do not grow negligent in keeping His commandments. When this impulse comes to you, remember that it comes from this interior dwelling place where God is in our soul, and praise Him very much. For certainly that note or letter is His, written with intense love and in such a way that He wants you alone to understand it and what He asks of you in it. By no means should you fail to respond to His Majesty, even though you may be externally occupied or in conversation with some persons. For it will often happen that our Lord will want to grant you this secret favor in public, and it is very easy—since the response is interior—to do what I'm saying and make an act of love, or say what St. Paul said: *Lord, what will You have me do?* In many ways He will teach you there what will be pleasing to Him and the acceptable time. I think it is understood that he hears us, and this touch, which is so delicate, almost always disposes the soul to be able to do what was said with a resolute will.

The difference in this dwelling place is the one mentioned: there are almost never any experiences of dryness or interior disturbance of the kind that were present at times in all the other dwelling places, but the soul is almost always in quiet. There is no fear that this sublime favor can be counterfeited by the devil, but the soul is wholly sure that the favor comes from God; for, as I have said, the faculties and senses have nothing to do with what goes on in this dwelling place. His Majesty reveals Himself to the soul and brings it to Himself in that place where, in my opinion, the devil will not dare enter, nor will the Lord allow him to enter. Nor does the Lord in all the favors He grants the soul here, as I have said, receive any assistance from the soul itself, except what it has already done in surrendering itself totally to God.

Every way in which the Lord helps the soul here, and all He teaches it, takes place with such quiet and so noiselessly that, seemingly to me, the work resembles the building of Solomon's temple where no sound was heard. So in this temple of God, in this His dwelling place, He alone and the soul rejoice together in the deepest silence. There is no reason for the intellect to stir or seek anything, for the Lord who created it wishes to give it repose here and that through a small crevice it might observe what is taking place. At times this sight is lost and the other faculties do not allow the intellect to look, but this happens for only a very short time. In my opinion, the faculties are not lost here; they do not work, but remain as though in amazement.

I am amazed as well to see that when the soul arrives here all raptures are taken away. Only once in a while are they experienced and then without those transports and that flight of the spirit. They happen very rarely and almost never in public as they very often did before. Nor do the great occasions of devotion cause the soul concern as previously. Nor, if souls in this dwelling place see a devout image or hear a sermon—previously it was almost as though they didn't hear it—or music, are they worried as was the poor little butterfly that went about so apprehensive that everything frightened it and made it fly. Now the reason could be that in this dwelling place either the soul has found its repose, or has seen so much that nothing frightens it, or that it doesn't feel that solitude it did before since it enjoys such company. In sum, Sisters, I don't know what the cause may be. For when the Lord begins to show what there is in this dwelling place and to bring the soul there, this great weakness is taken away. The weakness was a severe trial for the soul and previously was not taken away. Perhaps the reason is that the Lord has now fortified, enlarged, and made the soul capable. Or it could be that His Majesty wished to make known publicly that which He did with these souls in secret for certain reasons He knows, for His judgments are beyond all that we can imagine here below.

These effects, along with all the other good ones from the degrees of prayer we mentioned, are given by God when He brings the soul to Himself with this kiss sought by the bride, for I think this petition is here granted. Here an abundance of water is given to this deer that was wounded. Here one delights in God's tabernacle. Here the dove Noah sent out to see if the storm was over finds the olive branch as a sign of firm ground discovered amid the floods and tempests of this world. O Jesus! Who would know the many things there must be in Scripture to explain this peace of soul! My God, since You see how important it is for us, grant that Christians will seek it; and in Your mercy do not take it away from those to whom You have given it. For, in the end, people must always live with fear until You give them true peace and bring them there where that peace will be unending. I say "true peace," not because this peace is not true but because the first war could return if we were to withdraw from God.

But what will these souls feel on seeing that they could lack so great a blessing? Seeing this makes them proceed more carefully and seek to draw strength from their weakness so as not to abandon through their own fault any opportunity to please God more. The more favored they are by His Majesty the more they are afraid and fearful of themselves. And since through His grandeurs they have come to a greater knowledge of their own miseries, and their sins become more serious to them, they often go about like the publican not daring to raise their eyes. At other times they go about desiring to die so as to be safe; although, with the love they have, soon they again want to live in order to serve Him, as was said. And in everything concerning themselves they trust in His mercy. Sometimes the many favors make them feel more annihilated, for they fear that just as a ship too heavily laden sinks to the bottom they will go down too.

I tell you, Sisters, that the dross is not wanting but it doesn't disquiet or make them lose peace. For the storms, like a wave, pass quickly. And the fair weather returns, because the presence of the Lord they experience makes them soon forget everything. May He be ever blessed and praised by all His creatures, amen.

Questions

1. What blessings are brought by spiritual marriage?
2. What happens in the "seventh dwelling place" of God in the soul?
3. How can "peace" of soul be combined with experiencing suffering and persecution?

St. John of the Cross

Like St. Ignatius of Loyola and St. Teresa of Avila, St. John of the Cross (1542–1591) belongs to the extraordinary sixteenth-century flowering of the Church in Spain. With St. Teresa, he promoted the reform of the Carmelites in Spain. After entering the Carmelite order at age twenty-one, he spent the next few years studying philosophy and theology, particularly the work of St. Thomas Aquinas. Most of his writing was done late in his life, while also serving in various administrative capacities and as a spiritual director. The following excerpt is taken from his lengthy commentary on his poem "The Dark Night." In his commentary, he seeks to express the contemplative stages by which one attains union with God. The "dark night" is the period of purgation, of humbling, in which the soul is drawn away from all created things to God alone.

Book Two

Chapter 1

[The beginning of the treatise on the dark night of the spirit. Explains when this night commences.]

From *The Collected Works of St. John of the Cross*, translated by Kieran Kavanaugh and Otilio Rodriguez, 395–406. Copyright © 1964, 1979, 1991 by Washington Province of Discalced Carmelites, ICS Publications, 2131 Lincoln Road, N.E., Washington, DC, 20002-1199 U.S.A. www.icspublications.org.

If His Majesty intends to lead the soul on, he does not put it in this dark night of spirit immediately after its going out from the aridities and trials of the first purgation and night of sense. Instead, after having emerged from the state of beginners, the soul usually spends many years exercising itself in the state of proficients. In this new state, as one liberated from a cramped prison cell, it goes about the things of God with much more freedom and satisfaction of spirit and with more abundant interior delight than it did in the beginning before entering the night of sense. Its imagination and faculties are no longer bound to discursive meditation and spiritual solicitude, as was their custom. The soul readily finds in its spirit, without the work of meditation, a very serene, loving contemplation and spiritual delight. Nonetheless, the purgation of the soul is not complete. The purgation of the principal part, that of the spirit, is lacking, and without it the sensory purgation, however strong it may have been, is incomplete because of a communication existing between the two parts of the soul that form only one suppositum. As a result, certain needs, aridities, darknesses, and conflicts are felt. These are sometimes far more intense than those of the past and are like omens or messengers of the coming night of the spirit.

But they are not lasting, as they will be in the night that is to come. For after enduring the short period or periods of time, or even days, in this night and tempest, the soul immediately returns to its customary serenity. Thus God purges some individuals who are not destined to ascend to so lofty a degree of love as are others. He brings them into this night of contemplation and spiritual purgation at intervals, frequently causing the night to come and then the dawn so that David's affirmation might be fulfilled: *He sends his crystal* (contemplation) *like morsels* [Ps. 148:17]. These morsels of dark contemplation, though, are never as intense as is that frightful night of contemplation we are about to describe, in which God places the soul purposely in order to bring it to divine union.

The delight and interior gratification that these proficients enjoy abundantly and readily is communicated more copiously to them than previously and consequently overflows into the senses more than was usual before the sensory purgation. Since the sensory part of the soul is now purer, it can, after its own mode, experience the delights of the spirit more easily.

But since, after all, the sensory part of the soul is weak and incapable of vigorous spiritual communications, these proficients, because of such communications experienced in the sensitive part, suffer many infirmities, injuries, and weaknesses of stomach, and as a result fatigue of spirit. The Wise Man says: *The corruptible body is a load upon the soul* [Wis. 9:15]. Consequently the communications imparted to proficients cannot be very strong or very intense or very spiritual, as is required for divine union, because of the weakness and corruption of the senses that have their share in them.

Thus we have raptures and transports and the dislocation of bones, which always occur when the communications are not purely spiritual (communicated to the spirit alone) as are those of the perfect, who are already purified by the night of spirit. The perfect enjoy freedom of spirit without their senses being clouded or transported, for in them these raptures and bodily torments cease.

To point out why these proficients must enter this night of spirit, we will note some of their imperfections and some of the dangers they confront.

Chapter 2

[Other imperfections of these proficients.]

The imperfections in these proficients are of two kinds: habitual and actual. The habitual are the imperfect affections and habits still remaining like roots in the spirit, for the sensory purgation could not reach the spirit. The difference between the two purgations is like the difference between pulling up roots or cutting off a branch, rubbing out a fresh stain or an old, deeply embedded one. As we said, the purgation of the senses is only the gate to the beginning of the contemplation that leads to the purgation of spirit. This sensitive purgation, as we also explained, serves more for the accommodation of the senses to the spirit than for the union of the spirit with God. The stains of the old self still linger in the spirit, although they may not be apparent or perceptible. If these are not wiped away by the use of the soap and strong lye of this purgative night, the spirit will be unable to reach the purity of divine union.

These proficients also have the *hebetudo mentis*, the natural dullness everyone contracts through sin, and a distracted and inattentive spirit. The spirit must be illumined, clarified, and recollected by means of the hardships and conflicts of this night. All those who have not passed beyond the state of proficients possess these habitual imperfections that cannot, as we said, coexist with the perfect state of the union of love.

Not all these proficients fall into actual imperfections in the same way. Some encounter greater difficulties and dangers than those we mentioned, for their experience of these goods in the senses is so exterior and easily come by. They receive an abundance of spiritual communications and apprehensions in the sensory and spiritual parts of their souls and frequently behold imaginative and spiritual visions. All of this as well as other delightful feelings are the lot of those who are in this state, and a soul is often tricked through them by its own phantasy as well as by the devil. The devil finds it pleasing to suggest to souls and impress on them apprehensions and feelings. As a result of all this, these proficients are easily charmed and beguiled if they are not careful to renounce such apprehensions and feelings and energetically defend themselves through faith.

This is the stage in which the devil induces many into believing vain visions and false prophecies. He strives to make them presume that God and the saints speak with them, and frequently they believe their phantasy. It is here that the devil customarily fills them with presumption and pride. Drawn by vanity and arrogance, they allow themselves to be seen in exterior acts of apparent holiness, such as raptures and other exhibitions. They become audacious with God and lose holy fear, which is the key to and guardian of all the virtues. Illusions and deceptions so multiply in some, and they become so inveterate in them, that it is very doubtful whether they will return to the pure road of virtue and authentic spirituality. They fall into these miseries by being too secure in their surrender to these apprehensions and spiritual feelings, and do this just when they were beginning to make progress along the way.

So much could be said about the imperfections of these proficients and of how irremediable they are—since proficients think their blessings are more spiritual than formerly—that I desire to pass over the matter. I only assert, in order to establish the necessity of the spiritual night (the purgation) for anyone who is to advance, that no proficients, however strenuous their efforts, will avoid many of these natural affections and imperfect habits. These must be purified before one may pass on to divine union.

Furthermore, to repeat what was said above, these spiritual communications cannot be so intense, so pure, and so vigorous as is requisite for this union, because the lower part of the soul still shares in them. Thus, to reach union, the soul must enter the second night of the spirit.

In this night both the sensory and spiritual parts are despoiled of all these apprehensions and delights, and the soul is made to walk in dark and pure faith, which is the proper and adequate means to divine union as God says through Hosea: *I will espouse you* (unite you) *to me through faith* [Hos. 2:20].

Chapter 3

[An explanation for what is to follow.]

These souls, then, are not proficients. Their senses have been fed with sweet communications so that, allured by the gratification flowing from the spirit, they could be accommodated and united to the spirit. Each part of the soul can now in its own way receive nourishment from the same spiritual food and from the same dish of only one suppositum and subject. These two parts thus united and conformed are jointly prepared to suffer the rough and arduous purgation of the spirit that awaits them. In this purgation, these two portions of the soul will undergo complete purification, for one part is never adequately purged without the other. The real purgation of these senses begins with the spirit. Hence the night of the senses we explained should be called a certain reformation and bridling of the appetite rather than a purgation. The reason is that all the imperfections and disorders of the sensory part are rooted in the spirit and from it receive their strength. All good and evil habits reside in the spirit and until these habits are purged, the senses cannot be completely purified of their rebellions and vices.

In this night that follows both parts are jointly purified. This was the purpose of the reformation of the first night and the calm that resulted from it: that the sensory part, united in a certain way with the spirit, might undergo purgation and suffering with greater fortitude. Such is the fortitude necessary for so strong and arduous a purgation that if the lower part in its weakness is not reformed first, and afterward strengthened in God through the experience of sweet and delightful communion with him, it has neither the fortitude nor the preparedness to endure it.

These proficients are still very lowly and natural in their communication with God and in their activity directed toward him because the gold of the spirit is not purified and illumined. They still think of God and speak of him as little children, and their knowledge and experience of him is like that of little children, as St. Paul asserts [1 Cor. 13:11]. The reason is that they have not reached perfection, which is union of the soul with God. Through this union, as fully grown, they do mighty works in their spirit since their faculties and works are more divine than human, as we will point out. Wishing to strip them in fact of this old self and clothe them with the new, which is created according to God in the newness of sense, as the Apostle says [Col. 3:9–10; Eph. 4:22–24; Rom. 12:2], God divests the faculties, affections, and senses, both spiritual and sensory, interior and exterior. He leaves the intellect in darkness, the will in aridity, the memory in emptiness, and the affections in supreme affliction, bitterness, and anguish by depriving the soul of the feeling and satisfaction it previously obtained from spiritual blessings. For this privation is one of the conditions required that the spiritual form, which is the union of love, may be introduced into the spirit and united with it.

The Lord works all of this in the soul by means of a pure and dark contemplation, as is indicated in the first stanza. Although we explained this stanza in reference to the first night of the senses, the soul understands it mainly in relation to this second night of the spirit, since this night is the principal purification of the soul. With this in mind, we will quote it and explain it again.

Chapter 4

[The first stanza and its explanation.]

First Stanza
One dark night,
fired with love's urgent longings
—ah, the sheer grace!—
I went out unseen,
my house being now all stilled.

[Explanation.]
Understanding this stanza now to refer to contemplative purgation or nakedness and poverty of spirit (which are all about the same), we can thus explain it, as though the soul says:

Poor, abandoned, and unsupported by any of the apprehensions of my soul (in the darkness of my intellect, the distress of my will, and the affliction and anguish of my memory), left to darkness in pure faith, which is a dark night for these natural faculties, and with my will touched only by sorrows, afflictions, and longings of love of God, I went out from myself. That is, I departed from my low manner of understanding, and my feeble way of loving, and my poor and limited method of finding satisfaction in God. I did this unhindered by either the flesh or the devil.

This was great happiness and a sheer grace for me, because through the annihilation and calming of my faculties, passions, appetites, and affections, by which my experience and satisfaction in God were base, I went out from my human operation and way of acting to God's operation and way of acting. That is:

My intellect departed from itself, changing from human and natural to divine. For united with God through this purgation, it no longer understands by means of its natural vigor and light, but by means of the divine wisdom to which it was united. And my will departed from itself and became divine. United with the divine love, it no longer loves in a lowly manner, with its natural strength, but with the strength and purity of the Holy Spirit; and thus the will does not operate humanly in relation to God.

The memory, too, was changed into eternal apprehensions of glory.

And finally, all the strength and affections of the soul, by means of this night and purgation of the old self, are renewed with divine qualities and delights.

An explanation of the first verse follows:

One dark night,

Chapter 5

[Begins to explain how this dark contemplation is not only night for the soul but also affliction and torment.]

This dark night is an inflow of God into the soul, which purges it of its habitual ignorances and imperfections, natural and spiritual, and which the contemplatives call infused contemplation or mystical theology. Through this contemplation, God teaches the soul secretly and instructs it in the perfection of love without its doing anything or understanding how this happens.

Insofar as infused contemplation is loving wisdom of God, it produces two principal effects in the soul: by both purging and illumining, this contemplation prepares the soul for union with God through love. Hence the same loving wisdom that purges and illumines the blessed spirits purges and illumines the soul here on earth.

Yet a doubt arises: Why, if it is a divine light (for it illumines souls and purges them of their ignorance), does the soul call it a dark night? In answer to this, there are two reasons this divine wisdom is not only night and darkness for the soul but also affliction and torment. First, because of the height of the divine wisdom that exceeds the abilities of the soul; and on this account the wisdom is dark for the soul. Second, because of the soul's baseness and impurity; and on this account the wisdom is painful, afflictive, and also dark for the soul.

To prove the first reason, we must presuppose a certain principle of the Philosopher: that the clearer and more obvious divine things are in themselves, the darker and more hidden they are to the soul naturally. The brighter the light, the more the owl is blinded; and the more one looks at the brilliant sun, the more the sun darkens the faculty of sight, deprives and overwhelms it in its weakness.

Hence when the divine light of contemplation strikes a soul not yet entirely illumined, it causes spiritual darkness, for it not only surpasses the act of natural understanding but it also deprives the soul of this act and darkens it. This is why St. Dionysius and other mystical theologians call this infused contemplation a "ray of darkness"—that is, for the soul not yet illumined and purged. For this great supernatural light overwhelms the intellect and deprives it of its natural vigor.

David also said that clouds and darkness are near God and surround him [Ps. 18:11], not because this is true in itself, but because it appears thus to our weak intellects, which in being unable to attain so bright a light are blinded and darkened. Hence he next declared that clouds passed before the great splendor of his presence [Ps. 18:12], that is, between God and our intellect. As a result, when God communicates this bright ray of his secret wisdom to the soul not yet transformed, he causes thick darkness in its intellect.

It is also evident that this dark contemplation is painful to the soul in these beginnings. Since this divine infused contemplation has many extremely good properties, and the still unpurged soul that receives it has many extreme miseries, and because two contraries cannot coexist in one subject, the soul must necessarily undergo affliction and suffering. Because of the purgation of its imperfections caused by this contemplation, the soul becomes a battlefield in which these two contraries combat one another. We will prove this by induction in the following way.

In regard to the first cause of one's affliction: Because the light and wisdom of this contemplation is very bright and pure, and the soul in which it shines is dark and impure, a person will be deeply afflicted on receiving it. When eyes are sickly, impure, and weak, they suffer pain if a bright light shines on them.

The soul, because of its impurity, suffers immensely at the time this divine light truly assails it. When this pure light strikes in order to expel all impurity, persons feel so unclean and wretched that it seems God is against them and they are against God.

Because it seems that God has rejected it, the soul suffers such pain and grief that when God tried Job in this way it proved one of the worst of Job's trials, as he says: *Why have You set me against You, and I am heavy and burdensome to myself?* [Jb. 7:20]. Clearly beholding its impurity by means of this pure light, although in darkness, the soul understands distinctly that it is worthy neither of God nor of any creature. And what most grieves it is that it thinks it will never be worthy, and there are no more blessings for it. This divine and dark light causes deep immersion of the mind in the knowledge and feeling of one's own miseries and evils; it brings all these miseries into relief so the soul sees clearly that of itself it will never possess anything else. We can interpret that passage from David in this sense: *You have corrected humans because of their iniquity and have undone and consumed their souls, as a spider is eviscerated in its work* [Ps. 39:11].

Persons suffer affliction in the second manner because of their natural, moral, and spiritual weakness. Since this divine contemplation assails them somewhat forcibly in order to subdue and strengthen their soul, they suffer so much in their weakness that they almost die, particularly at times when the light is more powerful. Both the sense and the spirit, as though under an immense and dark load, undergo such agony and pain that the soul would consider death a relief. The prophet Job, having experienced this, declared: *I do not desire that he commune with me with much strength lest he overwhelm me with the weight of his greatness* [Jb. 23:6].

Under the stress of this oppression and weight, individuals feel so far from all favor that they think, and so it is, that even that which previously upheld them has ended, along with everything else, and there is no one who will take pity on them. It is in this sense that Job also cried out: *Have pity on me, at least you, my friends, for the hand of the Lord has touched me* [Jb. 19:21].

How amazing and pitiful it is that the soul be so utterly weak and impure that the hand of God, though light and gentle, should feel so heavy and contrary. For the hand of God does not press down or weigh on the soul, but only touches it; and this mercifully, for God's aim is to grant it favors and not to chastise it.

Chapter 6

[Other kinds of affliction suffered in this night.]

The two extremes, divine and human, which are joined here, produce the third kind of pain and affliction the soul suffers at this time. The divine extreme is the purgative contemplation, and the human extreme is the soul, the receiver of this contemplation. Since the divine extreme strikes in order to renew the soul and divinize it (by stripping it of the habitual affections and properties of the old self to which the soul is strongly united, attached, and conformed), it so disentangles and dissolves the spiritual substance—absorbing it in a profound darkness—that the soul at the sight of its miseries feels that it is melting away and being undone by a cruel spiritual death. It feels as if it were swallowed by a beast and being digested in the dark belly, and it suffers an anguish comparable to Jonah's in the belly of the whale [Jon. 2:1–3]. It is fitting that the soul be in this sepulcher of dark death in order that it attain the spiritual resurrection for which it hopes.

David describes this suffering and affliction—although it is truly beyond all description—when he says: *The sighs of death encircled me, the sorrows of hell surrounded me, in my tribulation I cried out* [Ps. 18:5–6].

But what the sorrowing soul feels most is the conviction that God has rejected it, and with abhorrence cast it into darkness. The thought that God has abandoned it is a piteous and heavy affliction for the soul. When David also felt this affliction he cried: *In the manner of the wounded, dead in the sepulchers, abandoned now by your hand so that you remember them no longer, so have you placed me in the deepest and lowest lake, in the darkness and shadow of death, and your wrath weighs on me, and all your waves you have let loose on me* [Ps. 88:4–7].

When this purgative contemplation oppresses a soul, it feels very vividly indeed the shadow of death, the sighs of death, and the sorrows of hell, all of which reflect the feeling of God's absence, of being chastised and rejected by him, and of being unworthy of him, as well as the object of his anger. The soul experiences all this and even more, for now it seems that this affliction will last forever.

Such persons also feel forsaken and despised by creatures, particularly by their friends. David immediately adds: *You have withdrawn my friends and acquaintances far from me; they have considered me an abomination* [Ps. 88:8]. Jonah, as one who also underwent this experience, both physically and spiritually in the belly of the whale, testifies: *You have cast me out into the deep, into the heart of the sea, and the current surrounded me; all its whirlpools and waves passed over me and I said: I am cast from the sight of your eyes; yet I shall see your holy temple again* (he says this because God purifies the soul that it might see his temple); *the waters encircled me even to the soul, the abyss went round about me, the open sea covered my head, I descended to the lowest parts of the mountains, the locks of the earth closed me up forever* [Jon. 2:4–7]. The "locks" refer to the soul's imperfections that hinder it from enjoying the delights of this contemplation.

Another excellence of dark contemplation, its majesty and grandeur, causes a fourth kind of affliction to the soul. This property makes the soul feel within itself the other extreme—its own intimate poverty and misery. Such awareness is one of the chief afflictions it suffers in the purgation.

The soul experiences an emptiness and poverty in regard to three classes of goods (temporal, natural, and spiritual) which are directed toward pleasing it, and is conscious of being placed in the midst of the contrary evils (the miseries of imperfections, aridities and voids in the apprehensions of the faculties, and an abandonment of the spirit in darkness).

Since God here purges both the sensory and spiritual substance of the soul, and its interior and exterior faculties, it is appropriately brought into emptiness, poverty, and abandonment in these parts, and left in dryness and darkness. For the sensory part is purified by aridity, the faculties by the void of their apprehensions, and the spirit by thick darkness.

God does all this by means of dark contemplation. And the soul not only suffers the void and suspension of these natural supports and apprehensions, which is a terrible anguish (like hanging in midair, unable to breathe), but it is also purged by this contemplation. As fire consumes the tarnish and rust of metal, this contemplation annihilates, empties, and consumes all the affections and imperfect habits the soul contracted throughout its life. Since these imperfections are deeply rooted in the substance of the soul, in addition to this poverty, this natural and spiritual emptiness, it usually suffers an oppressive undoing and an inner torment. Thus the passage of Ezekiel may be verified: *Heap together the bones, and I shall burn them in the fire, the flesh shall be consumed, and the whole composition burned, and the bones destroyed* [Ez. 24:10]. He refers here to the affliction suffered in the emptiness and poverty of both the sensory and the spiritual substance of the soul. And he then adds: *Place it also thus empty on the embers that its metal may become hot and melt and its uncleanness be taken away from it and its rust consumed* [Ez. 24:11]. This passage points out the heavy affliction the soul suffers from the purgation caused by the fire of this contemplation. For the prophet asserts that in order to burn away the rust of the affections the soul must, as it were, be annihilated and undone in the measure that these passions and imperfections are connatural to it.

Because the soul is purified in this forge *like gold in the crucible*, as the Wise Man says [Wis. 3:6], it feels both this terrible undoing in its very substance and extreme poverty as though it were approaching its end. This experience is expressed in David's cry: *Save me, Lord, for the waters have come even unto my soul; I am stuck in the mire of the deep, and there is nowhere to stand; I have come unto the depth of the sea, and the tempest has overwhelmed me. I have labored in crying out, my throat has become hoarse, my eyes have failed while I hope in my God* [Ps. 69:1–3].

God humbles the soul greatly in order to exalt it greatly afterward. And if he did not ordain that these feelings, when quickened in the soul, be soon put to sleep again, a person would die in a few days. Only at intervals is one aware of these feelings in all their intensity. Sometimes this experience is so vivid that it seems to the soul that it sees hell and perdition open before it. These are the ones who go down into hell alive [Ps. 55:15], since their purgation on earth is similar to what takes place there. For this purgation is what would have to be undergone there. The soul that endures it here on earth either does not enter that place, or is detained there for only a short while. It gains more in one hour here on earth by this purgation than it would in many there.

Questions

1. Is the "dark night," as described by St. John of the Cross, something experienced by beginners in prayer or people who do not pray?
2. Why is the dark night necessary? What prevents people from full union with God?
3. How does the dark night assist in our "divinization"?

Blessed John Henry Newman

Blessed John Henry Newman (1801–1890) began his career as an Anglican clergyman, theologian, and professor at Oxford. In 1845, he converted to Catholicism and became a priest of the Oratory of St. Philip Neri. Considered by many to be the greatest theologian of the nineteenth century, Newman was also a noted preacher. He preached the following sermon, taking as his text Hebrews 10:25, while an Anglican. He emphasizes that frequent public worship and devotions, not merely on Sundays, should be the norm in the Church. As opposed to privatized or individualistic understandings of the life of prayer, prayer belongs not only to the private life of the individual, but also, and centrally, to the public gathering of Christians.

"Not forsaking the assembling of ourselves together, as the manner of some is, but exhorting one another; and so much the more as ye see the Day approaching."

—Heb. x.25

THE FIRST CHRISTIANS SET UP THE CHURCH in continual prayer: "They persevering daily with one mind in the Temple, and breaking bread from house to house, did share their food with gladness and singleness

From "The Daily Service," in John Henry Newman, *Parochial and Plain Sermons* (San Francisco: Ignatius Press, 1988), 668–73.

of heart, praising God." St. Paul in his Epistles binds their example upon their successors for ever. Indeed, we could not have conceived, even if he and the other Apostles had been silent, that such a solemn opening of the Gospel, as that contained in the book of Acts, was only of a temporary nature, and not rather a specimen of what was to take place among the elect people in every age, and a shadow of that perfect service which will be their blessedness in heaven. However, St. Paul removes all doubt on this subject by expressly enjoining this united and unceasing prayer in various passages of his Epistles; as for instance, "I will . . . that men pray in every place, lifting up holy hands." "Persevere in prayer, and watch in the same with thanksgiving"; and in the text.

But it will be said, "Times are altered; the rites and observances of the Church are local and occasional; what was a duty then, need not be a duty now, even though St. Paul happens to enjoin it on those whom he addresses. Such continual prayer was the particular form which the religion of the early Christians took, and ours has taken another form." Do not suppose, because I allow myself thus to word the objection, that I therefore, for an instant, allow that continual united prayer may religiously be considered a mere usage or fashion; but so it is treated—so, perhaps, some of us in our secret hearts have at times been tempted to imagine; that is, we have been disposed to think that public worship at intervals of a week has in it something of natural fitness and reasonableness which continual weekday worship has not. Still, supposing it—granting daily worship to be a mere observance, or an usage, while Sunday worship is not—calling it by any title the most slighting and disparaging—the question returns, was this observance or usage of continual united prayer intended by the Apostles, for every age of the Church, or only for the early Christians? A precept may be but positive, not simply moral, and yet of perpetual obligation. Now, I answer confidently, that united prayer, unceasing prayer, is enjoined by St. Paul, in a passage just cited from an Epistle which lays down rules for the government and due order to the Church to the end of time. More plausibly even might we desecrate Sunday, which he does not mention in it, than neglect continual prayer, which he does. Observe how explicitly he speaks, "I will therefore that men pray in *every place*;"—not only at Jerusalem, not only at Corinth, not only in Rome, but even in England; in England at this day, in our secluded villages, in our rich populous busy towns, whatever be the importance of those secular objects which absorb our thoughts and time.

Or, again, take the text, and consider whether it favours the notion of a change or relaxation of the primitive custom. "Not forsaking the assembling of ourselves together, as the manner of some is, but exhorting one another; and so *much the more*, as ye see the Day approaching." The increasing troubles of the world, the fury of Satan, and the madness of the people, the dismay of sun, moon, and stars, distress of nations with perplexity, men's hearts failing them for fear, the sea and the waves roaring, all these gathering tokens of God's wrath are but calls upon us for greater perseverance in united prayer. Let those men especially consider this, who say that we are but dreaming of centuries gone by, missing our mark and born out of time, when we insist on such duties and practices as are now merely out of fashion; those who point to the tumult and the fever which agitates the whole nation, and say we must be busy and troubled too, in order to respond to it; who say that the tide of events has set in one way, and that we must give in to it, if we would be practical men; that it is idleness to attempt to stem a current, which it will be a great thing even to direct: that since the present age loves conversing and hearing about religion, and does not like silent thought, patient waiting, recurring prayers, severe exercises, that therefore we must obey it, and, dismissing rites and sacraments, convert the Gospel into a rational faith, so called, and a religion of the heart; let these men seriously consider St. Paul's exhortation, that we are to persevere in prayer—and that in every place—and the more, the more troubled and perplexed the affairs of this world become; not indeed omitting active exertions, but not, on that account, omitting prayer.

I have spoken of St. Paul, but, consider how this rule of "continuing in prayer" is exemplified in St. Peter's history also. He had learned from his Saviour's pattern not to think prayer a loss of time. Christ had taken him up with Him into the holy mount, though multitudes waited to be healed and taught below. Again, before His passion, He had taken him into the garden of Gethsemane; and while He prayed Himself, He called upon him likewise to "watch and pray lest he entered into temptation." In consequence, St. Peter warns us in his Epistle, as St. Paul in the text, "The end of all things is at hand, be ye therefore sober, and watch unto prayer." And, in one memorable passage of his history, he received a revelation of a momentous and most gracious truth, when he was at his prayers. Who would not have said that he was wasting his time, when he retired to the house of Simon at Joppa, for many days, and went up upon the house-top to pray, about the sixth hour? Was that, it might be asked, the part of an Apostle, whose commission was to preach the Gospel? Was he thus burying his light, instead of meeting the exigencies of the time? Yet, there God met him, and put a word in his mouth. There he learned the comfortable truth that the Gentiles were no longer common or unclean, but admissible into the Covenant of Grace. And if continual prayer was the employment of an Apostle, much more was it observed by those Christians who were less prominently called to labour. Accordingly, when St. Peter was in prison, prayers were offered for him, "without ceasing," by the Church; and to those prayers he was granted. When miraculously released, and arrived at the house of Mary, the mother of Mark, he found "many gathered together praying."

Stated and continual prayer, then, and especially united prayer, is plainly the duty of Christians. And if we ask how often we are to pray, I reply, that we ought to consider prayer as a plain privilege, directly we know that it is a duty, and therefore that the question is out of place. Surely, when we know we may approach the Mercy-seat, the only further question is, whether there be anything to forbid us coming often, anything implying that such frequent coming is presumptuous and irreverent. So great a mercy is it to be permitted to come, that a humble mind may well ask, "Is it a profane intrusion to come when I will?" If it be not, such a one will rejoice to come continually. Now, by way of removing these fears, Scripture contains most condescending intimations that we may come at all times. For instance, in the Lord's Prayer petition is made for *daily* bread for *this* day; therefore, our Saviour intended it should be used daily. Further, it is said, "give *us*," "forgive *us*," therefore it may fairly be presumed to be given us as a social prayer. Thus in the Lord's Prayer itself there seems to be sanction for daily united prayer. Again, if we consider His words in the parable, twice a day at least seems permitted us, "Shall not God avenge His own elect, which cry day and night unto Him?" though this is to take the words according to a very restricted interpretation. And since Daniel prayed three times a day, and the Psalmist even seven, under the Law, we may infer, that Christians, certainly, are not irreverent, nor incur the blame of using vain repetitions, though they join in many Services.

Now, I do not see what can be said in answer to these arguments, imperfect as they are compared with the whole proof that might be adduced, except that some of the texts cited may, perhaps, refer to mere secret prayer almost without words, and some speak primarily of private prayer. Yet it is undeniable, on the other hand, that united prayer, not private or secret, is principally intended in those passages of the New Testament, which speak of prayer at all; and if so, the remainder may be left to apply indirectly or not, as we chance to decide, without interfering with a conclusion otherwise drawn. If, however, it be said that family prayer is a fulfillment of the duty, without prayer in Church, I reply, that I am not at all speaking of it as a duty, but as a privilege; I do not tell men that they must come to Church, so much as declare the glad tidings that they may. This surely is enough for those who "hunger and thirst after righteousness," and humbly desire to see the face of God.

Now, I will say a few words on the manner in which the early Christians fulfilled this duty.

Quite at first, when the persecutions raged, they assembled when and where they could. At times they could but avail themselves of Christ's promise, that if two of his disciples "*agree* on earth, as touching anything that they shall ask, it shall be done for them of their Heavenly Father," though, by small parties, and in the towns, they seem to have met together continually from the first. Gradually, as they grew stronger, or as they happened to be tolerated, they made full proof of their sacred privilege, and showed what was the desire of their hearts.

Their most solemn Service took place on the Lord's day, as might be expected, when the Holy Eucharist was celebrated. Next to Sunday came Wednesday and Friday, when, also assemblies for worship continued till three o'clock in the afternoon, and were observed with fasting; in some places with the Eucharist also. Saturday, too, was observed in certain branches of the Church with special devotion, the Holy Mysteries being solemnized and other Services performed as on the Lord's day.

Next must be mentioned, the Festivals of the Martyrs, when, in addition to the sacred Services used on the Lord's day, there was read some account of the particular Martyr commemorated, with exhortations to follow his pattern.

These holydays, whether Sunday or Saint's day, were commonly ushered in by a Vigil or religious watching, as you find it noted down in the Calendar at the beginning of the Prayer-Book. These lasted through the night.

Moreover, there were the sacred Seasons, such as the forty days of Lent for fasting, and the fifty days between Easter and Whitsuntide for rejoicing.

Such was the course of special devotions in the early Church; but, besides, every day had its ordinary Services, viz., prayer morning and evening.

Besides these, might be mentioned the prayers at the canonical hours, which were originally used for private, but, at length, for united worship; viz., at the third hour, or nine in the morning, in commemoration of the Holy Ghost's descent at Pentecost at that hour; at the sixth, the time of St. Peter's vision at Joppa, in memory of our Saviour's crucifixion; and at the ninth, in memory of His death, which was the hour when St. Peter and St. John went up to the Temple and healed the lame man. It may be added that in some places the Holy Eucharist was celebrated and partaken daily.

This is by no means a full enumeration of the sacred Services in the early Church; but it is abundantly sufficient for my purpose, which is to show how highly they valued the privilege of united prayer, and how literally they understood the words of Christ and His Apostles. I am by no means contending, that every point of discipline and order in this day must be precisely the same as it was then. Christians then had more time on their hands than many of us have; and certain peculiarities of the age and place might combine to allow them to do what we cannot do. Still, so far must be clear to every candid person who considers the state of the case, that they found some sort of pleasure in prayer which we do not; that they took delight in an exercise, which—(I am afraid I must say, though it seems profane even to say it)—which we should consider painfully long and tedious.

This too is worth observing of the primitive Christians, that they united social and private prayer in their Service. On holydays, for instance, when it was extended till three o'clock in the afternoon, they commenced with singing the Psalms, in the midst of which two Lessons were read, as is usual with us, commonly one from the Old and one from the New Testament. But in some places, instead of these Lessons, after every Psalm, a short space was allowed for private prayer to be made in silence, much in the way we say a short prayer on coming into and going out of Church. After the Psalms and Lessons came the Sermon, the more solemn prayers having not yet begun. Shortly after, followed the celebration of the Holy Communion, which again was introduced by a time of silence for private prayer, such as we at this day are allowed during the administration of the Sacred Elements to other communicants.

And in this way lengthened out and varied their Services; principally, that is, by means of private prayers and psalms: so that, when no regular course of service was proceeding, yet the Church might be full of people, praying in secret and confessing their sins, or singing together psalms or hymns. Thus exactly did they fulfill the Scripture precepts— "Is any among you afflicted? let him pray; is any merry? let him sing psalms," and "Let the word of Christ dwell in you richly in all wisdom; teaching and admonishing one another in psalms and hymns and spiritual songs, singing with grace in your hearts to the Lord."

Questions

1. What are the advantages of frequent communal prayer and worship?
2. How does Newman trace frequent communal prayer in the New Testament and the early Church?
3. How do we value holy days?

Blessed Elizabeth of the Trinity

Blessed Elizabeth of the Trinity belongs to the period of flowering of the Church in France in the late nineteenth century. A Carmelite like her contemporary St. Therese of Lisieux, Blessed Elizabeth of the Trinity died in 1906 at age twenty-six in the Carmel at Dijon, France, which she had entered only five years earlier. Known for her doctrine of "heaven on earth," desiring to be in the presence of God at all times and to rejoice continually in the holy Trinity even in the midst of earthly labors, Blessed Elizabeth emphasizes in her writings the indwelling of the Trinity in our souls. The text included here is her Last Retreat, in which she guides us into the joys of life in Christ. Her style is to draw on her wide reading of Scripture and of spiritual writers and, by piecing together key insights, present her own profound spiritual vision for how to live.

First Day

First Prayer

"FATHER, I WILL THAT WHERE I AM they also whom You have given Me may be with Me, because You have loved Me before the creation of

From *The Complete Works Elizabeth of the Trinity*, vol. 1, translated by Sr. Aletheia Kane, O.C.D., 94–113. Copyright © 1984 by Washington Province of Discalced Carmelites, ICS Publications, 2131 Lincoln Road, N.E., Washington, DC, 20002-1199 U.S.A. www.icspublications.org.

the world." Such is Christ's last wish, His supreme prayer before returning to His Father. He wills that where He is we should be also, not only
for eternity, but already in time, which is eternity begun and still in
progress. It is important then to know where we must live with Him in
order to realize His divine dream. "The place where the Son of God is
hidden is the bosom of the Father, or the divine Essence, invisible to
every mortal eye, unattainable by every human intellect," as Isaiah said:
"Truly You are a hidden God." And yet His will is that we should be established in Him, that we should live where He lives, in the unity of love;
that we should be, so to speak, His own shadow.

By baptism, says St. Paul, we have been united to Jesus Christ. And
again: "God seated us together in Heaven in Christ Jesus, that He might
show in the ages to come the riches of His grace." And further on: "You
are no longer guests or strangers, but you belong to the City of saints
and the House of God." The Trinity—this is our dwelling, our "home,"
the Father's house that we must never leave. The Master said one day:
"The slave does not remain with the household forever, but the son remains there forever" (St. John).

Second Prayer

"Remain in Me." It is the Word of God who gives this order, expresses
this wish. Remain in Me, not for a few moments, a few hours which must
pass away, but "*remain . . .*" permanently, habitually, Remain in Me, pray
in Me, adore in Me, love in Me, suffer in Me, work and act in Me. Remain
in Me so that you may be able to encounter anyone or anything; penetrate further still into these depths. This is truly the "solitude into which
God wants to allure the soul that He may speak to it," as the prophet sang.

In order to understand this very mysterious saying, we must not, so to
speak, stop at the surface, but enter ever deeper into the divine Being
through recollection. "I pursue my course," exclaimed St. Paul; so must
we descend daily this pathway of the Abyss which is God; let us slide
down this slope in wholly loving confidence. "Abyss calls to abyss." It is
there in the very depths that the divine impact takes place, where the
abyss of our nothingness encounters the Abyss of mercy, the immensity
of the all of God. There we will find the strength to die to ourselves and,
losing all vestige of self, we will be changed into love. . . . "Blessed are
those who die in the Lord"!

Second Day

First Prayer

"The kingdom of God is within you." A while ago God invited us to "remain in Him," to live spiritually in His glorious heritage, and now He reveals to us that we do not have to go out of ourselves to find Him: "The kingdom of God is within"! . . . St. John of the Cross says that "it is in the substance of the soul where neither the devil nor the world can reach" that God gives Himself to it; then "all its movements are divine, and although they are from God they also belong to the soul, because God works them in it and with it."

The same saint also says that "God is the center of the soul. So when the soul with all" its "strength will know God perfectly, love and enjoy Him fully, then it will have reached the deepest center that can be attained in Him." Before attaining this, the soul is already "in God who is its center," "but it is not yet in its *deepest* center, for it can still go further. Since love is what unites us to God, the more intense this love is, the more deeply the soul enters into God and the more it is centered in Him. When it 'possesses even one degree of love it is already in its center'; but when this love has attained its perfection, the soul will have penetrated into its *deepest* center. There it will be transformed to the point of becoming very like God." To this soul living within can be addressed the words of Père Lacordaire to St. Mary Magdalene: "No longer ask for the Master among those on earth or in Heaven, for He is your soul and your soul is He."

Second Prayer

"Hurry and come down, for I must stay in your house today." The Master unceasingly repeats this word to our soul which He once addressed to Zacchaeus. "Hurry and come down." But what is this descent that He demands of us except an entering more deeply into our interior abyss? This act is not "an external separation from external things," but a "solitude of spirit," a detachment from all that is not God.

"As long as our will has fancies that are foreign to divine union, whims that are now yes, now no, we are like children; we do not advance with giant steps in love for fire has not yet burnt up all the alloy; the gold is not pure; we are still seeking ourselves; God has not consumed" all our hostility to Him. But when the boiling cauldron has consumed "every imperfect love, every imperfect sorrow, every imperfect fear," "then love is perfect and the golden ring of our alliance is larger than Heaven and earth. This is the secret cellar in which love places his elect," this "love leads us by ways and paths known to him alone; and he leads us with no turning back, for we will not retrace our steps."

Third Day

First Prayer

"If anyone loves Me, he will keep My word and My Father will love him, and We will come to him and make our home *in him*."

The Master once more expresses His desire to dwell in us. "If anyone loves Me"! It is love that attracts, that draws God to His creatures: not a sensible love but that love "strong as death that deep waters cannot quench."

"Because I love My Father, I do always the things that are pleasing to Him." Thus spoke our holy Master, and every soul who wants to live close to Him must also live this maxim. The divine good pleasure must be its food, its daily bread; it must let itself be immolated by all the Father's wishes in the likeness of His adored Christ. Each incident, each event, each suffering, as well as each joy, is a sacrament which gives God to it; so it no longer makes a distinction between these things; it surmounts them, goes beyond them to rest in its Master, above all things. It "exalts" Him high on the "mountain of its heart," yes, "higher than His gifts, His consolation, higher than the sweetness that descends from Him." "The property of love is never to seek self, to keep back nothing, but to give everything to the one it loves." "Blessed the soul that loves" in truth; "the Lord has become its captive through love"!

Second Prayer

"You have died and your life is hidden with Christ in God." St. Paul comes to bring us a light to guide us on the pathway of the abyss. "You have died!" What does that mean but that the soul that aspires to live close to God "in the invincible fortress of holy recollection" must be "set apart, stripped, and withdrawn from all things" (*in spirit*). This soul "finds within itself a simple ascending movement of love to God, whatever creatures may do; it is invincible to things which" pass away, "for it transcends them, seeking God alone."

"Quotidie morior." "I die daily." I decrease, I renounce self more each day so that Christ may increase in me and be exalted; I "remain" very little "in the depths of my poverty." I see "my nothingness, my misery, my weakness; I perceive that I am incapable of progress, of perseverance; I see the multitude of my shortcomings, my defects; I appear in my indigence." "I fall down in my misery, confessing my distress, and I display it before the mercy" of my Master. "Quotidie morior." I place the joy of my soul (as to the will, not sensible feelings) in everything that can immolate, destroy, or humble me, for I want to make room for my Master. I live no longer I, but He lives in me: I no longer want "to live my own life, but to be transformed in Jesus Christ so that my life may be more divine than human," so that the Father in bending attentively over me can recognize the image of His beloved Son in whom He has placed all His delight.

Fourth Day

First Prayer

"Deus ignis consumens." Our God, wrote St. Paul, is a consuming Fire, that is "a fire of love" which destroys, which "transforms into itself everything that it touches." "The delights of the divine enkindling are renewed in our depths by an unremitting activity: the enkindling of love in a mutual and eternal satisfaction. It is a renewal that takes place at every moment in the bond of love." Certain souls "have chosen this refuge to rest there eternally, and this is the silence in which, somehow, they have lost themselves." "Freed from their prison, they sail on the Ocean of Divinity without any creature being an obstacle or hindrance to them."

For these souls, the mystical death of which St. Paul spoke yesterday becomes so simple and sweet! They think much less of the work of destruction and detachment that remains for them to do than of plunging into the Furnace of love burning within them which is no one other than the Holy Spirit, the same Love which in the Trinity is the bond between the Father and His Word. They "enter into Him by living faith, and there, in simplicity and peace" they are "carried away by Him" beyond all things, beyond sensible pleasures, "into the sacred darkness" and are "transformed into the divine image." They lie, in St. John's expression, in "communion" with the Three adorable Persons, "sharing" their life, and this is "the contemplative life"; this contemplation "leads to possession." "Now this simple possession is eternal life savored in the unfathomable abode. It is there, beyond reason, that the profound tranquility of the divine immutability awaits us."

Second Prayer

"I have come to cast fire upon the earth and how I long to see it burn." It is the master Himself who expresses His desire to see the fire of love enkindled. In fact, "all our works and all our labors are nothing in His sight. We can neither give Him anything nor satisfy His only desire, which is to exalt the dignity of our soul." Nothing pleases Him so much as to see it "grow." "Now nothing can exalt it so much as to become in some way the equal of God; that is why He demands from the soul the tribute of its love, as the property of love is to make the lover equal to the beloved as much as possible. The soul in possession of this love" "appears on an equal footing with Christ because their mutual affection renders everything common to both." "I have called you My friends because all things that I have heard from My Father I have made known to you."

But to attain to this love the soul must first be "entirely surrendered," its "will must be calmly lost in God's will" so that its "inclinations," "its faculties" "move only in this love and for the sake of this love. I do everything with love, I suffer everything with love: this is what David meant when he sang, 'I will keep all my strength for You.'" Then "love fills it so completely, absorbs it and protects it" so well "that everywhere it finds the secret of growing in love," "even in its relations with the world"; "in the midst of life's cares it can rightly say: 'My only occupation is loving'! . . .'"

Fifth Day

First Prayer

"Behold, I stand at the door and knock. If any man listens to My voice and opens the door to Me, I will come in to him and sup with him, and he with Me." Blessed the ears of the soul alert enough, recollected enough to hear this voice of the Word of God; blessed also the eyes of this soul which in the light of a deep and living faith can witness the "coming" of the Master into His intimate sanctuary. But what then is this coming? "It is an unceasing generation, an enduring hymn of praise." Christ "comes with His treasures, but such is the mystery of the divine swiftness that He is continually coming, always for the first time as if He had never come; for His coming, independent of time, consists in an eternal "*now*," and an eternal desire eternally renews the joys of the coming. The delights that He brings are infinite, since they are Himself." "The capacity of the soul, enlarged by the coming of the Master, seems to go out of itself in order to pass through the walls into the immensity of Him who comes; and a phenomenon occurs: God, who is in our depths, receives God coming to us, and God contemplates God! God in whom beatitude consists."

Second Prayer

"He who eats My flesh and drinks My blood, remains in Me and I in him." "The first sign of love is this: that Jesus has given us His flesh to eat and His blood to drink." "The property of love is to be always giving and always receiving. Now the love" of Christ is "generous. All that He has, all that He is, He gives; all that we have, all that we are, He takes away. He asks for more than we of ourselves are capable of giving. He has an immense hunger which wants to devour us absolutely. He enters even into the marrow of our bones, and the more lovingly we allow Him to do so, the more fully we savor Him." "He knows that we are poor, but He pays no heed to it and does not spare us. He Himself becomes in us His own bread, first burning up, in His love, all our vices, faults, and sins. Then when He sees that we are pure, He comes like a gaping vulture that is going to devour everything. He wants to consume our life in order to change it into His own; ours, full of vices, His, full of grace and glory and all prepared for us, if only we will renounce ourselves. Even if our eyes were good enough to see this avid appetite of Christ who hungers for our salvation, all our efforts would not prevent us from disappearing into His open mouth." Now "this sounds absurd, but those who love will understand!" When we receive Christ "with interior devotion, His blood, full of warmth and glory, flows into our veins and a fire is enkindled in our depths." "We receive the likeness of His virtues, and He lives in us and we in Him. He gives us His soul with the fullness of grace, by which the soul perseveres in love and praise of the Father"! "Love draws its object into itself; we draw Jesus into ourselves; Jesus draws us into Himself. Then carried above ourselves into love's interior," seeking God, "we go to meet Him, to meet His Spirit, which is His love, and this love burns us, consumes us, and draws us into unity where beatitude awaits us." "Jesus meant this when He said: 'With great desire have I desired to eat this pasch with you.'"

Sixth Day

First Prayer

"To approach God we must believe." Thus speaks St. Paul. He also says, "Faith is the substance of things to be hoped for, the evidence of things not seen." That is, "faith makes so present and so certain future goods, that by it, they take on existence in our soul and subsist there before we have fruition of them." St. John of the Cross says that it serves as "feet" to go "to God," and that it is "possession in an obscure manner." "It alone can give us true light" concerning Him whom we love, and our soul must "choose it as the means to reach blessed union." "It pours out in torrents in the depths of our being all spiritual goods. Christ, speaking to the Samaritan woman, indicated faith when He promised to all those who would believe in Him that He would given them 'a fountain of water springing up unto life everlasting.'" "Thus even in this life faith gives us God, covered, it is true, with a veil but nonetheless God Himself." "When that which is perfect comes," that is, clear vision, then "that which is imperfect," in other words, knowledge given through faith, "will receive all its perfection."

"We have come to know and to believe in the love God has for us." That is our great act of faith, the way to repay our God love for love; it is "the mystery hidden" in the Father's heart, of which St. Paul speaks, which, at last, we penetrate and our whole soul thrills! When it can believe in this "exceeding love" which envelops it, we may say of it as was said of Moses, "He was unshakable in faith as if he had seen the Invisible." It no longer rests in inclinations or feelings; it matters little to the soul whether it feels God or not, whether He sends it joy or suffering: it believes in His love. The more it is tried, the more its faith increases because it passes over all obstacles, as it were, to go rest in the heart of infinite Love who can perform only works of love. So also to this soul wholly awakened in its faith the Master's voice can say in intimate secrecy the words He once addressed to Mary Magdalene: "Go in peace, your faith has saved you."

Second Prayer

"If your eye is single, your whole body will be full of light." What is this single eye of which the Master speaks but this "simplicity of intention" which "gathers into unity all the scattered forces of the soul and unites the spirit itself to God. It is simplicity which gives God honor and praise; it is simplicity which presents and offers the virtues to Him. Then, penetrating and permeating itself, permeating and penetrating all creatures, it finds God in its depths. It is the principle and end of virtues, their splendor and their glory. I call simplicity of intention that which seeks only God and refers all things to Him." "This is what places man in the presence of God; it is simplicity that gives him light and courage; it is simplicity that empties and frees the soul from all fear today and on the day of judgment." "It is the interior slope" and "the foundation of the whole spiritual life." "It crushes evil nature under foot, it gives peace, it imposes silence on the useless noises within us." It is simplicity that "hourly increases our divine likeness. And then, without the aid of intermediaries, it is simplicity again that will transport us into the depths where God dwells and will give us the repose of the abyss. The inheritance which eternity has prepared for us will be given us by simplicity. All the life of the spirits, all their virtue, consists—with the divine likeness—in simplicity, and their final rest is spent on the heights in simplicity also." "And according to the measure of its love, each spirit possesses a more or less profound search for God in its own depths." The simple soul, "rising by virtue of its interior gaze, enters into itself and contemplates in its own abyss the sanctuary where it is touched" by the touch of the Holy Trinity. Thus it has penetrated into its depths "to the very foundation which is the gate of life eternal."

Seventh Day

First Prayer

"God chose us in Him before creation, that we should be holy and immaculate in His presence, in love."

"The Holy Trinity created us in its image, according to the eternal design that it possessed in its bosom before the world was created," in this "beginning without beginning" of which Bossuet speaks following St. John: "In principio erat Verbum." In the beginning was the Word; and we could add: in the beginning was nothing, for God in His eternal solitude already carried us in His thought. "The Father contemplates Himself" "in the abyss of His fecundity, and by the very act of comprehending Himself He engendered another person, the Son, His eternal Word. The archetype of all creatures who had not yet issued out of the void eternally dwelt in Him, and God saw them and contemplated them in their type in Himself. This eternal life which our archetypes possessed without us in God, is the cause of our creation."

"Our created essence asks to be rejoined with its principle." The Word, "the Splendor of the Father, is the eternal archetype after which creatures are designed on the day of their creation." This is "why God wills that, freed from ourselves, we should stretch out our arms towards our exemplar and possess it," "rising" above all things "towards our model." "This contemplation opens" the soul "to unexpected horizons." "In a certain manner it possesses the crown towards which it aspires." "The immense riches that God possesses by nature, we may possess by virtue of love, by His dwelling in us and by our dwelling in Him." "It is by virtue of this immense love" that we are drawn into the depths of the "intimate sanctuary" where God "imprints on us a true image of His majesty." Thus it is, thanks to love and through love, as the Apostle says, that we can be holy and immaculate in God's presence, and can sing with David: "I will be unblemished and I will guard myself from the depths of sinfulness within me."

Second Prayer

"Be holy for I am holy." It is the Lord who speaks. "Whatever may be our way of life or the clothing we wear, each of us must be the holy one of God." Who then is "the most holy"? "The one who is most loving, who gazes longest on God and who most fully satisfies the desires of His gaze." How do we satisfy the desires of God's gaze but by remaining "simply and lovingly" turned towards Him so that He may reflect His own image as the sun is reflected through a pure crystal. "Let us make man in our own image and likeness": such was the great desire in the Heart of our God. "Without the likeness which comes from grace, eternal damnation awaits us. When God sees that we are prepared to receive His grace, His generous goodness is ready to give us the gift that will give us His likeness. Our aptitude for receiving His grace depends on the inner integrity with which we move towards Him." And then God, "bringing us His gifts," can "give Himself, imprint on us His likeness, forgive and free us."

"The highest perfection in this life," says a pious author, "consists in remaining so closely united to God that the soul with all its faculties and its powers is recollected in God," "that its affections united in the joy of love find rest only in possession of the Creator. The image of God imprinted in the soul is formed by reason, memory, and will. As long as these faculties do not bear the perfect image of God, they do not resemble Him as on the day of creation. The form of the soul is God who must imprint Himself there like the seal on wax, like the stamp on its object. Now this is not fully realized unless the intellect is completely enlightened by knowledge of God, the will captivated by love of the supreme good, and the memory fully absorbed in contemplation and enjoyment of eternal happiness." "And as the glory of the blessed is nothing else than the perfect possession of this state, it is obvious that the initial possession of these blessings constitutes perfection in this life." To "realize this ideal" we must "keep recollected within ourselves," "remain silently in God's presence," "while the soul immerses itself, expands, becomes enkindled and melts in Him, with an unlimited fullness."

Eighth Day

First Prayer

"Those whom God has foreknown, He has also predestined to become conformed to the image of His divine Son. . . . And those whom He has predestined, He has also called; and those whom He has called He has also justified; and those whom He has justified He has also glorified.

What then shall we say after that? If God is for us, who can be against us? . . . Who will separate me from the love of Christ?" This is how the mystery of predestination, the mystery of divine election appeared to the enlightened gaze of the Apostle. "Those whom He has foreknown." Are not we of that number? Cannot God say to our soul what He once said through the voice of His prophet: "I passed by you and saw you. I saw that the time had come for you to be loved. I spread my garment over you. I swore to you to protect you, and I made a covenant with you, and you became mine."

Yes, we have become His through baptism, that is what Paul means by these words: "He called them"; yes, called to receive the seal of the Holy Trinity; at the same time we have been made, in the words of St. Peter, "sharers in the divine nature," we have received "a beginning of His existence." . . . Then, He has justified us by His sacraments, by His direct "touches" in our contemplation "in the depths" of our soul; justified us also by faith and according to the measure of our faith in the redemption that Jesus Christ has acquired for us. And finally, He wants to glorify us, and for that reason, says St. Paul, He "has made us worthy to share in the inheritance of the saints in light," but we will be glorified in the measure in which we will have been conformed to the image of His divine Son. So let us contemplate this adored Image, let us remain unceasingly under its radiance so that it may imprint itself on us; let us go to everything with the same attitude of soul that our holy Master would have. Then we will realize the great plan by which God has "resolved in Himself to restore all things in Christ."

Second Prayer

"It seems to me that all is loss since I have known the excelling knowledge of my Lord Jesus Christ. For love of Him I have forfeited everything. I have accounted all else rubbish that I may gain Christ. What I want is to know Him, to share in His sufferings, to become like Him in His death. I pursue my course striving to attain what He has destined me for by taking hold of me. My whole concern is to forget what is behind and to strain forward constantly to what is ahead. I run straight to the goal, to the vocation to which God has called me in Christ Jesus." That is: I want only to be identified with Him: "Mihi vivere Christus est," "Christ is my life!"

All the intensity of St. Paul's soul is poured out in these lines. The object of this retreat is to make us more like our adored Master, and even more, to become so one with Him that we may say: "I live no longer I, but He lives in me. And the life that I now live in this body of death, I live in the faith of the Son of God, who loved me and gave Himself up for me." Oh! Let us study this divine Model: His knowledge, the Apostle tells us, is so "excelling."

And when He first came into the world what did He say? "You no longer delight in holocausts; so I have assumed a body and I come, O God, to do Your will." During the thirty-three years of His life this will became so completely His daily bread, that at the moment of handing over His soul into His Father's hands, He could say to Him: "All is accomplished," yes, all Your desires, *all* have been realized, that is why "I have glorified You on earth." When Jesus Christ spoke to His apostles of this food which they did not know, He explained to them "that it was to do the will of Him who sent Me." Also He could say: "I am never alone. He who sent Me is always with Me because I do always the things that are pleasing to Him."

Let us lovingly eat this bread of the will of God. If sometimes His will is more crucifying, we can doubtless say with our adored Master: "Father, if it is possible, let this cup pass me by," but we will add immediately: "Yet not as I will, but as You will"; and in strength and serenity, with the divine Crucified, we will also climb our calvary singing in the depths of our hearts and raising a hymn of thanksgiving to the Father. For those who march on this way of sorrows are those "whom He foreknew and predestined to be conformed to the image of His divine Son," the One crucified by love!

Ninth Day

First Prayer

"God has predestined us to the adoption of children through Jesus Christ, in union with Him, according to the decree of His will, to make the glory of His grace blaze forth, by which He has justified us in His beloved Son. In whose blood we have redemption, the remission of our sins, according to the riches of His grace, which has abounded beyond measure in us in all wisdom and prudence. . . ." "The soul now a true daughter of God is, in the words of the Apostle, moved by the Holy Spirit Himself: 'All who are led by the Spirit of God are children of God.'" And again: "We have not received a spirit of slavery to be still led by fear, but the spirit of adoption as children in which we cry out: Abba, Father! The Spirit Himself gives witness with our spirit that we are children of God. But if we are children, we are heirs as well; I mean heirs of God and co-heirs with Jesus Christ if only we suffer with Him so as to be glorified with Him." "It is to bring us to this abyss of glory that God has created us in His image and likeness."

"See," says St. John, "what manner of love the Father has bestowed on us, that we should be called children of God; and such we are. . . . Now we are the children of God, and we have not yet seen what we shall be. We know that when He appears, we shall be like Him, for we shall see Him just as He is. And everyone who has this hope in Him makes himself holy, just as He Himself is holy."

This is the measure of the holiness of the children of God: "to be holy as God, to be holy with the holiness of God"; and we do this by living close to Him in the depths of the bottomless abyss "within." "Then the soul seems in some way to resemble God Who, even though He delights in all things, yet does not delight in them as much as He does in Himself, for He possesses within Himself a supereminent good before which all others disappear. Thus all the joys which the soul receives are so many reminders inviting her to enjoy by preference the good she already possesses and to which nothing else can compare." "Our Father Who art in Heaven. . . ." It is in "this little heaven" that He has made in the center of our soul that we must seek Him and above all where we must remain.

Christ said one day to the Samaritan woman that "the Father seeks true adorers in spirit and truth." To give joy to His Heart, let us be these true adorers. Let us adore Him in "spirit," that is, with our hearts and our thoughts fixed on Him, and our mind filled with His knowledge imparted the light of faith. Let us adore Him in "truth," that is, by our works for it is above all by our actions that we show we are true: this is to do always what is pleasing to the Father whose children we are. And finally, let us "adore in spirit and in truth," that is, *through* Jesus Christ and with Jesus Christ, for He alone is the true Adorer in spirit and truth.

Then we will be daughters of God; we will "know with an experiential knowledge the truth of these words of Isaiah: 'You will be carried at the breast and He will caress you on His knees.'" In fact "God seems to be wholly occupied with overwhelming the soul with caresses and marks of affection like a mother who brings up her child and feeds it with her own milk." Oh! Let us be attentive to the mysterious voice of our Father! "My daughter," He says, "give Me your heart."

Second Prayer

"God who is rich in mercy, impelled by His exceeding love, even when we were dead because of our sins, has brought us back to life in Christ Jesus. . . ." "Because all have sinned and have need of the glory of God, they are justified freely by His grace, through the redemption which is in Christ, whom God has set forth as a propitiation for sins, showing both that He is just and that He makes just him who has *faith* in Him" (St. Paul).

"Sin is such a terrifying evil that in order to seek any good whatsoever, or to avoid any evil whatsoever, no sin should be committed." "Now we have committed very many." How can we keep from "fainting in adoration when we plunge into the abyss of mercy and the eyes of our soul are fixed upon this fact: God has taken away our sins." He said so Himself: "I will blot out all their iniquities and I will no longer remember their sins."

"The Lord, in His mercy, willed to turn our sins against themselves to our advantage; He found a way to make them useful for us, to convert them in our hands into a means of salvation. But do not let this diminish in any way our horror of sinning, nor our sorrow for having sinned. But our sins" "have become a source of humility for us."

When the soul "considers deep within itself, its eyes burning with love, the immensity of God, His fidelity, the proofs of His love, His favors which can add nothing to His happiness; then, looking at itself it sees its crimes against this immense Lord, it turns to its own center with such self-contempt that it does not know how it can endure its horror." "The best thing for it to do is to complain to God, its Friend, of the strength of its self-love which betrays it by not letting it place itself as low as it would wish. It resigns itself to the will of God, and in self-abnegation, finds true, invincible, and perfect peace, which nothing can disturb. For it has plunged into such a deep abyss that no one will seek it there."

"If anyone should affirm to me that to find the bottom of the abyss is to be immersed in humility, I would not contradict him. However, it seems to me that to be plunged into humility is to be plunged into God, for God is the bottom of the abyss. That is why humility, like charity, is always capable of increasing." "Since a humble heart is the vessel needed, the vessel capable of containing the grace God wants to pour into it," let us be "humble." "The humble can never rank God high enough nor themselves low enough. But here is the wonder: their weakness turns into wisdom, and the imperfection of their acts, always insufficient in their eyes, will be the greatest delight of their life. Whoever possesses humility has no need of many words to be instructed; God tells him more things than he can learn; such was the case with the Lord's disciples."

Tenth Day

First Prayer

"Si scires donum Dei. . . ." "If you knew the gift of God," Christ said one evening to the Samaritan woman. But what is this gift of God if not Himself? And, the beloved disciple tells us: "He came to His own and His own did not accept Him." St. John the Baptist could still say to many souls these words of reproach: "There is one in the midst of you, *'in you,'* whom you do not know."

"If you knew the gift of God. . . ." There is one who knew this gift of God, one who did not lose one particle of it, one who was so pure, so luminous that she seemed to be the Light itself: "Speculum justitiae." One whose life was so simple, so lost in God that there is hardly anything we can say about it.

"Virgo fidelis": that is, Faithful Virgin, "who kept all these things in her heart." She remained so little, so recollected in God's presence, in the seclusion of the temple, that she drew down upon herself the delight of the Holy Trinity: "Because He has looked upon the lowliness of His servant, henceforth all generations shall call me blessed!" The Father bending down to this beautiful creature, who was so unaware of her own beauty, willed that she be the Mother in time of Him whose Father He is in eternity. Then the Spirit of love who presides over all of God's works came upon her; the Virgin said her *fiat*: "Behold the servant of the Lord, be it done to me according to Your word," and the greatest of mysteries was accomplished. By the descent of the Word in her, Mary became forever God's prey.

It seems to me that the attitude of the Virgin during the months that elapsed between the Annunciation and the Nativity is the model for interior souls, those whom God has chosen to live within, in the depths of the bottomless abyss. In what peace, in what recollection Mary lent herself to everything she did! How even the most trivial things were divinized by her! For through it all the Virgin remained the adorer of the gift of God! This did not prevent her from spending herself outwardly when it was a matter of charity; the Gospel tells us that Mary went in haste to the mountains of Judea to visit her cousin Elizabeth. Never did the ineffable vision that she contemplated within herself in any way diminish her outward charity. For, a pious author says, if contemplation "continues towards praise and towards the eternity of its Lord, it possesses unity and will not lose it. If an order from Heaven arrives, contemplation turns towards men, sympathizes with their needs, is inclined towards all their miseries; it must cry and be fruitful. It illuminates like fire, and like it, it burns, absorbs and devours, lifting up to Heaven what it has devoured. And when it has finished its work here below, it rises, burning with its fire, and takes up again the road on high."

Second Prayer

"We have been predestined by the decree of Him who works all things according to the counsel of His will, so that we may be *the praise of His glory.*"

It is St. Paul who tells us this, St. Paul who was instructed by God Himself. How do we realize this great dream of the Heart of our God, this immutable will for our souls? In a word, how do we correspond to our vocation and become perfect *Praises of Glory* of the Most Holy Trinity?

"In Heaven" each soul is a praise of glory of the Father, the Word, and the Holy Spirit, for each soul is established in pure love and "lives no longer its own life, but the life of God." Then it knows Him, St. Paul says, as it is known by Him. In other words, "its intellect is the intellect of God, its will the will of God, its love the very love of God. In reality it is the Spirit of love and of strength who transforms the soul, for to Him it has been given to supply what is lacking to the soul," as St. Paul says again. "He works in it this glorious transformation." St. John of the Cross affirms that "the soul surrendered to love, through the strength of the Holy Spirit, is not far from being raised to the degree of which we have just spoken," even here below! This is what I call a perfect praise of glory!

A praise of glory is a soul that lives in God, that loves Him with a pure and disinterested love, without seeking itself in the sweetness of this love; that loves Him beyond all His gifts and even though it would not have received anything from Him, it desires the good of the Object thus loved. Now how do we *effectively* desire and will good to God if not in accomplishing His will since this will orders everything for His greater glory? Thus the soul must surrender itself to this will completely, passionately, so as to will nothing else but what God wills.

A praise of glory is a soul of silence that remains like a lyre under the mysterious touch of the Holy Spirit so that He may draw from it divine harmonies; it knows that suffering is a string that produces still more beautiful sounds; so it loves to see this string on its instrument that it may more delightfully move the Heart of its God.

A praise of glory is a soul that gazes on God in faith and simplicity; it is a reflector of all that He is; it is like a bottomless abyss into which He can flow and expand; it is also like a crystal through which He can radiate and contemplate all His perfections and His own splendor. A soul which thus permits the divine Being to satisfy in itself His need to communicate "all that He is and all that He has," is in reality the praise of glory of all His gifts.

Finally, a praise of glory is one who is always giving thanks. Each of her acts, her movements, her thoughts, her aspirations, at the same time that they are rooting her more deeply in love, are like an echo of the eternal Sanctus.

In the Heaven of glory the blessed have no rest "day or night, saying: Holy, holy, holy is the Lord God Almighty. . . . They fall down and worship Him who lives forever and ever. . . ."

In the heaven of her soul, the praise of glory has already begun her work of eternity. Her song is uninterrupted, for she is under the action of the Holy Spirit who effects everything in her; and although she is not always aware of it, for the weakness of nature does not allow her to be established in God without distractions, she always sings, she always adores, for she has, so to speak, wholly passed into praise and love in her passion for the glory of her God. In the heaven of our soul let us be praises of glory of the Holy Trinity, praises of love of our Immaculate

Mother. One day the veil will fall, we will be introduced into the eternal courts and there we will sing in the bosom of infinite Love. And God will give us "the new name promised to the Victor." What will it be?

LAUDEM GLORIAE

Questions

1. "Abyss calls to abyss." How does Blessed Elizabeth interpret these words?
2. Why make room for Christ in our souls?
3. Describe the importance of simplicity.

St. Edith Stein

St. Edith Stein, born into a devout Jewish family in Poland in 1891, studied philosophy under the famous phenomenologist Edmund Husserl and Max Scheler. After reading St. Teresa of Avila, she converted to Catholicism in 1922, giving up her university post as Husserl's assistant. In 1933, she entered the Carmelite convent at Cologne and took the name Sister Teresa Benedicta of the Cross. In 1938, due to Nazi persecution of the Jews in Germany, she moved to the Carmel at Echt in the Netherlands; but when the Dutch bishops spoke out against Hitler's anti-Semitism, Hitler responded by intensifying his persecution of religious leaders and Jews in the Netherlands. St. Edith Stein was arrested and died in the gas chamber at Auschwitz in 1942, a victim of the Holocaust. The following selection is taken from a lecture given by St. Edith Stein to her Carmelite sisters, in which she illumines the relationship of Jesus Christ and his Church to the Old Testament and describes the varieties of prayer and praise of God that are the hidden sources of renewal.

"THROUGH HIM, WITH HIM, and in him in the unity of the Holy Spirit, all honor and glory is yours, Almighty Father, for ever and ever."

From *The Hidden Life*, translated by Waltraut Stein, Ph.D., 7–13, 15–17. Copyright © 1992 by Washington Province of Discalced Carmelites, ICS Publications, 2131 Lincoln Road, N.E., Washington, DC, 20002-1199 U.S.A. www .icspublications.org.

With these solemn words, the priest ends the Eucharistic prayer at the center of which is the mysterious event of the consecration. These words at the same time encapsulate the prayer of the church: honor and glory to the triune God through, with, and in Christ. Although the words are directed to the Father, all glorification of the Father is at the same time glorification of the Son and of the Holy Spirit. Indeed, the prayer extols the majesty that the Father imparts to the Son and that both impart to the Holy Spirit from eternity to eternity.

All praise of God is *through, with,* and *in* Christ. *Through* him, because only through Christ does humanity have access to the Father and because his existence as God-man and his work of salvation are the fullest glorification of the Father; *with* him, because all authentic prayer is the fruit of union with Christ and at the same time buttresses this union, and because in honoring the Son one honors the Father and vice versa; *in* him, because the praying church is Christ himself, with every individual praying member as a part of his Mystical Body, and because the Father is in the Son and the Son the reflection of the Father, who makes his majesty visible. The dual meanings of *through, with,* and *in* clearly express the God-man's mediation.

The prayer of the church is the prayer of the ever-living Christ. Its prototype is Christ's prayer during his human life.

1. The Prayer of the Church as Liturgy and Eucharist

The Gospels tell us that Christ prayed the way a devout Jew faithful to the law prayed. Just as he made pilgrimages to Jerusalem at the prescribed times with his parents as a child, so he later journeyed to the temple to celebrate the high feasts there with his disciples. Surely he sang with holy enthusiasm along with his people the exultant hymns in which the pilgrim's joyous anticipation streamed forth: "I rejoiced when I heard them say: Let us go to God's house" (Ps. 122:1). From his last supper with his disciples, we know that Jesus said the old blessings over bread, wine, and the fruits of the earth, as they are prayed to this day. So he fulfilled one of the most sacred religious duties: the ceremonial Passover seder to commemorate deliverance from slavery in Egypt. And perhaps this very gathering gives us the most profound glimpse into Christ's prayer and the key to understanding the prayer of the church.

While they were at supper, he took bread, said the blessing, broke the bread, and gave it to his disciples, saying, "Take this, all of you, and eat it: this is my body which will be given up for you."

In the same way, he took the cup, filled with wine. He gave you thanks, and giving the cup to his disciples, said, "Take this, all of you, and drink from it: this is the cup of my blood, the blood of the new and everlasting covenant. It will be shed for you and for all so that sins may be forgiven."

Blessing and distributing bread and wine were part of the Passover rite. But here both receive an entirely new meaning. This is where the life of the church begins. Only at Pentecost will it appear publicly as a Spirit-filled and visible community. But here at the Passover meal the seeds of the vineyard are planted that make the outpouring of the Spirit possible. In the mouth of Christ, the old blessings become life-giving words. The fruits of the earth become his body and blood, filled with his life. Visible creation, which he entered when he became a human being, is now united with him in a new, mysterious way. The things that serve to sustain human life are fundamentally transformed, and the people who partake of them in faith are transformed too, drawn into the unity of life with Christ and filled with his divine life. The Word's life-giving power is bound to the sacrifice. The Word became flesh in order to surrender the life he assumed, to offer himself and a creation redeemed by his sacrifice in praise to the Creator. Through the Lord's last supper, the Passover meal of the Old Covenant is converted into the Easter meal of the New Covenant: into the sacrifice on the cross at Golgotha and those joyous meals between Easter and Ascension when the disciples recognized the Lord in the breaking of bread, and into the sacrifice of the Mass with Holy Communion.

As the Lord took the cup, he gave thanks. This recalls the words of blessing thanking the Creator. But we also know that Christ used to give thanks when, prior to a miracle, he raised his eyes to his Father in heaven. He gives thanks because he knows in advance that he will be heard. He gives thanks for the divine power that he carries in himself and by means of which he will demonstrate the omnipotence of the Creator to human eyes. He gives thanks *for* the work of salvation that he is permitted to accomplish, and *through* this work, which is in fact itself the glorification of the triune Godhead, because it restores this Godhead's distorted image to pure beauty. Therefore the whole perpetual sacrificial offering of Christ—at the cross, in the holy Mass, and in the eternal glory of heaven—can be conceived as a single great thanksgiving—as Eucharist: as gratitude for creation, salvation, and consummation. Christ presents himself in the name of all creation, whose prototype he is and to which he descended to renew it from the inside out and lead it to perfection. But he also calls upon the entire created world itself, united with him, to give the Creator the tribute of thanks that is his due. Some understanding of this Eucharistic character of prayer had already been revealed under the Old Covenant. The wondrous form of the tent of meeting, and later, of Solomon's temple, erected as it was according to divine specifications, was considered an image of the entire creation, assembled in worship and service around its Lord. The tent around which the people of Israel camped during their wanderings in the wilderness was called the "home of God among us" (Exod. 38:21). It was thought of as a "home below," in contrast to a "higher home." "O Lord, I love the house where you dwell, the place where your glory abides," sings the Psalmist (Ps. 26:8), because the tent of meeting is "valued as much as the creation of the world." As the heavens in the creation story were stretched out like a carpet, so carpets were prescribed as walls for the tent. As the waters of the earth were separated from the waters of the heavens, so the curtain separated the Holy of Holies from the outer rooms. The "bronze" sea is modeled after the sea that is contained by its shores. The seven-branched light in the tent stands for the heavenly lights. Lambs and birds stand for the swarms of life teeming in the water, on the earth, and in the air. And as the earth is handed over to people, so in the sanctuary there stands the high priest "who is purified to act and to serve before God." Moses blessed, anointed, and sanctified the completed house as the Lord blessed and sanctified the work of his hands on the seventh day. The Lord's house was to be a witness to God on earth just as heaven and earth are witnesses to him (Deut. 30:19).

In place of Solomon's temple, Christ has built a temple of living stones, the communion of saints. At its center, he stands as the eternal high priest; on its altar he is himself the perpetual sacrifice. And, in turn, the whole of creation is drawn into the "liturgy," the ceremonial worship service: the fruits of the earth as the mysterious offerings, the flowers and the lighted candlesticks, the carpets and the curtain, the ordained priest, and the anointing and blessing of God's house. Not even the cherubim are missing. Fashioned by the hand of the artist, the visible forms stand watch beside the Holy of Holies. And, as living copies of them, the "monks resembling angels" surround the sacrificial altar and make sure that the praise of God does not cease, as in heaven so on earth. The solemn prayers they recite as the resonant mouth of the church frame the holy sacrifice. They also frame, permeate, and consecrate all other "daily work," so that prayer and work become a single *opus Dei*, a single "liturgy." Their readings from the holy Scriptures and from the fathers, from the menologies of the church and the teachings of its principal pastors, are a great, continually swelling hymn of praise to the rule of providence and to the progressive actualization of the eternal plan of salvation. Their morning hymns of praise call all of creation together to unite once more in praising the Lord: mountains and hills, streams and rivers, seas and lands and all that inhabit them, clouds and winds, rain and snow, all peoples of the earth, every class and race of people, and finally also the inhabitants of heaven, the angels and the saints. Not only in representations giving them human form and made by human hands are they to participate in the general Eucharist of creation, but they are to be involved as personal beings—or better, we are to unite ourselves through our liturgy to their eternal praise of God. . . .

2. Solitary Dialogue with God as the Prayer of the Church

The individual human soul a temple of God—this opens to us an entirely new, broad vista. The prayer life of Jesus was to be the key to understanding the prayer of the church. We saw that Christ took part in the public and prescribed worship services of his people, i.e., in what one usually calls "liturgy." He brought the liturgy into the most intimate relationship with his sacrificial offering and so for the first time gave it its full and true meaning—that of thankful homage of creation to its Creator. This is precisely how he transformed the liturgy of the Old Covenant into that of the New.

But Jesus did not merely participate in public and prescribed worship services. Perhaps even more often the Gospels tell of solitary prayer in the still of the night, on open mountain tops, in the wilderness far from people. Jesus' public ministry was preceded by forty days and forty nights of prayer. Before he chose and commissioned his twelve apostles, he withdrew into the isolation of the mountains. By his hour on the Mount of Olives, he prepared himself for his road to Golgotha. A few

short words tell us what he implored of his Father during this most difficult hour of his life, words that are given to us as guiding stars for our
own hours on the Mount of Olives. "Father, if you are willing, take this
cup away from me. Nevertheless, let your will be done, not mine." Like
lightning, these words for an instant illumine for us the innermost spiritual life of Jesus, the unfathomable mystery of his God-man existence
and his dialogue with the Father. Surely, this dialogue was life-long and
uninterrupted. Christ prayed interiorly not only when he had withdrawn from the crowd, but also when he was among people. And once
he allowed us to look extensively and deeply at this secret dialogue. It
was not long before the hour of the Mount of Olives; in fact, it was immediately before they set out to go there at the end of the Last Supper,
which we recognize as the actual hour of the birth of the church. "Having loved his own, . . . he loved them to the end." He knew that this was
their last time together, and he wanted to give them as much as he in any
way could. He had to restrain himself from saying more. But he surely
knew that they could not bear any more, in fact, that they could not even
grasp this little bit. The Spirit of Truth had to come first to open their
eyes for it. And after he had said and done everything that he could say
and do, he lifted his eyes to heaven and spoke to the Father in their presence. We call these words Jesus' great high priestly prayer, for this talk-
ing alone with God also had its antecedent in the Old Covenant. Once a
year on the greatest and most holy day of the year, on the Day of Atonement, the high priest stepped into the Holy of Holies before the face of
the Lord "to pray for himself and his household and the whole congregation of Israel." He sprinkled the throne of grace with the blood of a
young bull and a goat, which he previously had to slaughter, and in this
way absolved himself and his house "of the impurities of the sons of Israel and of their transgressions and of all their sins." No person was to
be in the tent (i.e., in the holy place that lay in front of the Holy of
Holies) when the high priest stepped into God's presence in this awe-
somely sacred place, this place where no one but he entered and he himself only at this hour. And even now he had to burn incense "so that a
cloud of smoke . . . would veil the judgment throne . . . and he not die."
This solitary dialogue took place in deepest mystery.

The Day of Atonement is the Old Testament antecedent of Good Friday. The ram that is slaughtered for the sins of the people represents the
spotless Lamb of God (so did, no doubt, that other—chosen by lot and

burdened with the sins of the people—that was driven into the wilderness). And the high priest descended from Aaron foreshadows the eternal high priest. Just as Christ anticipated his sacrificial death during the last supper, so he also anticipated the high priestly prayer. He did not have to bring for himself an offering for sin because he was without sin. He did not have to await the hour prescribed by the Law, nor to seek out the Holy of Holies in the temple. He stands, always and everywhere, before the face of God; his own soul is the Holy of Holies. It is not only God's dwelling, but is also essentially and indissolubly united to God. He does not have to conceal himself from God by a protective cloud of incense. He gazes upon the uncovered face of the Eternal One and has nothing to fear. Looking at the Father will not kill him. And he unlocks the mystery of the high priest's realm. All who belong to him may hear how, in the Holy of Holies of his heart, he speaks to his Father; they are to experience what is going on and are to learn to speak to the Father in their own hearts.

The Savior's high priestly prayer unveils the mystery of the inner life: the circumincession of the Divine Persons and the indwelling of God in the soul. In these mysterious depths the work of salvation was prepared and accomplished itself in concealment and silence. And so it will continue until the union of all is actually accomplished at the end of time. The decision for the Redemption was conceived in the eternal silence of the inner divine life. The power of the Holy Spirit came over the Virgin praying alone in the hidden, silent room in Nazareth and brought about the Incarnation of the Savior. Congregated around the silently praying Virgin, the emergent church awaited the promised new outpouring of the Spirit that was to quicken it into inner clarity and fruitful outer effectiveness. In the night of blindness that God laid over his eyes, Saul awaited in solitary prayer the Lord's answer to his question, "What do you want me to do?" In solitary prayer Peter was prepared for his mission to the Gentiles. And so it has remained all through the centuries. In the silent dialogue with their Lord of souls consecrated to God, the events of church history are prepared that, visible far and wide, renew the face of the earth. The Virgin, who kept every word sent from God in her heart, is the model for such attentive souls in whom Jesus' high priestly prayer comes to life again and again. And women who, like her, were totally self-forgetful because they were steeped in the life and suffering of Christ, were the Lord's preferred choice as instruments to accomplish great things in the church: a St. Bridget, a Catherine of Siena. And when St. Teresa, the powerful reformer of her Order at a time of widespread falling away from the faith, wished to come to the rescue of the church, she saw the renewal of true interior life as the means toward this end. . . .

3. Inner Life and Outer Form and Action

The work of salvation takes place in obscurity and stillness. In the heart's quiet dialogue with God the living building blocks out of which the kingdom of God grows are prepared, the chosen instruments for the construction forged. The mystical stream that flows through all centuries is no spurious tributary that has strayed from the prayer life of the church—it is its deepest life. When this mystical stream breaks through traditional forms, it does so because the Spirit that blows where it will is living in it, this Spirit that has created all traditional forms and must ever create new ones. Without him there would be no liturgy and no church. Was not the soul of the royal psalmist a harp whose strings resounded under the gentle breath of the Holy Spirit? From the overflowing heart of the Virgin Mary blessed by God streamed the exultant hymn of the "Magnificat." When the angel's mysterious word became visible reality, the prophetic "Benedictus" hymn unsealed the lips of the old priest Zechariah, who had been struck dumb. Whatever arose from spirit-filled hearts found expression in words and melodies and continues to be communicated from mouth to mouth. The "Divine Office" is to see that it continues to resound from generation to generation. So the mystical stream forms the many-voiced, continually swelling hymn of praise to the triune God, the Creator, the Redeemer, and the Perfecter. Therefore, it is not a question of placing the inner prayer free of all traditional forms as "subjective" piety in contrast to the liturgy as the "objective" prayer of the church. All authentic prayer is prayer of the church. Through every sincere prayer something happens in the church, and it is the church itself that is praying therein, for it is the Holy Spirit living in the church that intercedes for every individual soul "with sighs too deep for words." This is exactly what "authentic" prayer is, for "no one can say 'Jesus is Lord' except by the Holy Spirit." What could the prayer of the church be, if not great lovers giving themselves to God who is love!

The unbounded loving surrender to God and God's return gift, full and enduring union, this is the highest elevation of the heart attainable, the highest level of prayer. Souls who have attained it are truly the heart of the church, and in them lives Jesus' high priestly love. Hidden with Christ in God, they can do nothing but radiate to other hearts the divine love that fills them and so participate in the perfection of all into unity in God, which was and is Jesus' great desire.

Questions

1. Compare the Passover and the Eucharist.
2. Does prayer make an impact in the world's history?
3. In what way is the Virgin Mary a model of prayer?

Index

About the Editor

Matthew Levering is associate professor of theology at Ave Maria University in Naples, Florida. His other volumes in this series include *On the Priesthood, On Christian Dying*, and *On Marriage and Family.* He has authored *Scripture and Metaphysics* and *Christ's Fulfillment of Torah and Temple* and is the coauthor of *Knowing the Love of Christ* and *Holy People, Holy Land.* He has most recently edited *Reading John with St. Thomas Aquinas.* He serves as coeditor of the theological quarterly *Nova et Vetera.*